THE CHURCH-RELATED PRE-SCHOOL

MARGARET CHASTAIN REED

Published by
ABINGDON PRESS/NASHVILLE

THE CHURCH-RELATED PRESCHOOL

Copyright © 1985 by Abingdon Press

All rights reserved.
No part of this book may be reproduced in any manner whatsoever without written permission of the publisher except brief quotations embodied in critical articles or reviews. For information address Abingdon Press, Nashville, Tennessee.

Library of Congress Cataloging in Publication Data

REED, MARGARET CHASTAIN, 1926–
The church-related preschool.
(A Griggs educational resource)
Bibliography: p.
1. Education, Preschool—United States.
2. Church schools—United States. I. Title.
LB1140.23.R44   1985   372'.21   84-16755

ISBN 0-687-08334-6

MANUFACTURED BY THE PARTHENON PRESS AT
NASHVILLE, TENNESSEE, UNITED STATES OF AMERICA

To the Teachers at
The Pines

CONTENTS

FOREWORD   7

PREFACE   9

INTRODUCTION   11

CONSIDERING A WEEKDAY PROGRAM   19

THE WEEKDAY PROGRAM—A PART OF THE CHURCH   26

SETTING UP AN ADMINISTRATIVE BOARD   29
   Goal Setting   30
   Determining Policies   31
   Costs of Starting a Weekday Program   39
   Meeting Licensing Standards   41
   The Work of the Board   42
   Common Misconceptions   44

THE DIRECTOR   50
   The Director's Relationship to the Board   50
   The Director's Needs   52
   Leadership Styles   55
   Writing a Job Description for the Director   57
   Program Evaluation   59

TEACHERS   61
   Steps in Hiring   66
   Working with Teachers   69
   Teachers' Needs   73
   Evaluation of Teachers   77
   Solving Staff Problems   80

WORKING WITH PARENTS 82
   Teacher-Parent Conferences 86
   Confidentiality 91
   Notes That Go Home 91
   Parent Meetings 92

CONCLUSION 95

FOREWORD

Child care programs for preschool children are an important factor in the way America is raising its children today. Though parents have in no measure given up their rights or responsibilities as parents, child care in all its forms has provided them with a valuable resource in the child-rearing process.

A surprising number of these programs have found their way into the nation's churches. In fact, according to a recent study conducted by the National Council of Churches of Christ, the church may be the single largest provider of child care in the country.

While there is no simple answer to the question of why the church has become so involved in child day care, local parishes have certain unique features that make them particularly desirable locations for child care programs: available space, convenient community location, and tax-exempt status.

Classrooms originally designed for Sunday school groups have child-size fittings and furnishings which are essential for child care programs. This ideal space is generally available for child day care programs because most parishes use the facilities only for a few hours on Sunday or on other infrequent occasions when child care and education are offered to parents otherwise engaged in the life and worship of the church.

The convenience of church space for child care provision is further enhanced by the location of the church within the community. The church's universal presence creates a network of institutions that reaches deep into the life of all types of American communities. No matter how small the town, at least one church structure can be assured. Whatever a community's patterns and preferences for residence and employment, a church is close at hand: close to public transportation, along major city streets, nestled among housing projects.

In addition to their physical space and location, the churches offer an important financial advantage for provision of child care because of their exemption from taxes. Tax exemption provides a general reduction in overhead costs. One experienced child care provider says, "Even when other doors are closed in a community, churches will at least consider housing child care centers. The problems and start-up costs associated with opening are usually sharply reduced because the church already has equipment, insurance, and garbage collection. If the church is willing, the child care program can operate under the church's non-profit status."

Thus, space, location, and tax-exempt status all contribute to the desirability of church properties for child care programs. For these reasons alone some churches find themselves involved in the provision of child care, yet we must look far beyond these factors to explain the extent of the church's role as provider. Thousands of churches in hamlets, towns, and cities have made a conscious decision to respond to the needs of young children and their families. For some, this has meant the establishment of community nursery schools; of comprehensive day care programs for infants, toddlers, preschoolers, and young schoolage children; or of programs for migrant children or children with disabilities. For others, this response has resulted in a preschool program offered part-day and reflecting Christian attitudes and values. These programs will find this book most beneficial. Margaret Reed has produced a valuable, step-by-step guide for those who have accepted the challenge for such a ministry.

Through programs of preschool education, congregations are offered the opportunity and challenged by the Holy Spirit to faithfully witness to the wholeness of the gospel. Child care ministries provide one area in which the evangelical, educational, and social justice ministries of the church can be integrated and offered to children and their families. Indeed, if Margaret Reed is correct, we can scarcely do less.

The Reverend Eileen W. Lindner
Director, Child Advocacy Office
National Council of the Churches of Christ
New York, 1984

PREFACE

How wonderful it is that we have the ability to learn from others and from the situations in which we find ourselves! As I look back over past experiences, many persons come to mind who have contributed to making this book possible.

Ruth McNielly, former head teacher at the University of Kansas Laboratory Nursery School, repeatedly demonstrated the value of technique in working with children.

I have never met Katherine H. Read, but her books have been an inspiration and I have used them frequently for teacher training. Dorothy Baruch's book on discipline has also much influenced my thinking.

I have known for a long time that the people who work in our churches' weekday programs for young children have problems and concerns that are unique to their situation. I have learned much from their questions and comments as I have worked with them.

I am especially indebted to the teachers and members of The Pines Presbyterian Church for all they have taught me.

Linda Lebsack, Kitty Clark, and Marianna Reed have spent many hours in manuscript preparation, and I am very appreciative.

This book would not have been possible without the encouragement and help of Roland Tapp and Patricia Griggs.

Margaret Chastain Reed

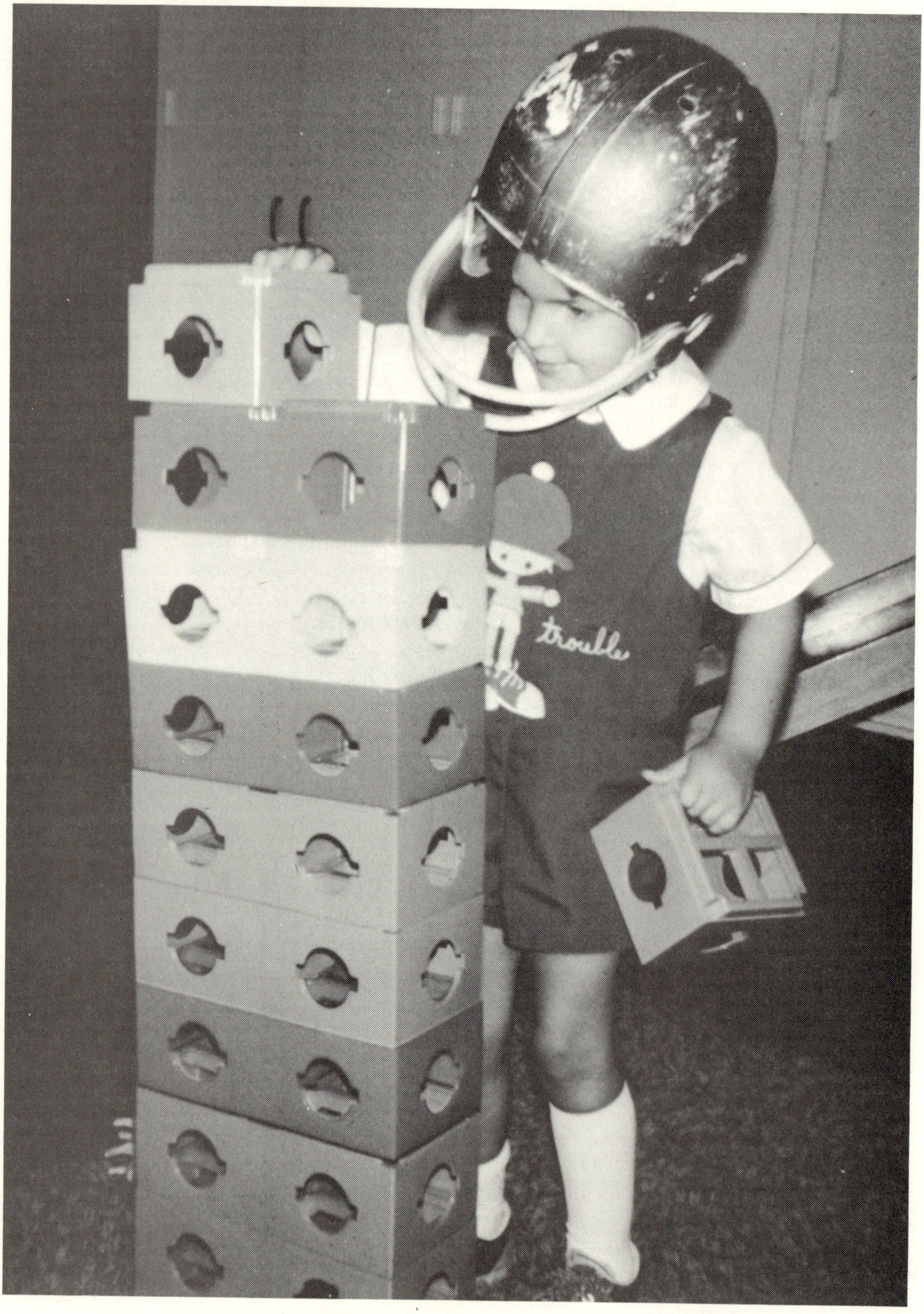
trouble

INTRODUCTION

The days are long gone when a church sat idle during the week, a giant sleeping edifice, unused, dark, and waiting for Sunday to come to breathe life into its timbers. A Sunday school classroom could once keep its curriculum pictures and posters on the walls, and chairs and tables in their appropriate spots, from noon of one Sunday until 9:30 A.M. of the next.

The church's thrust has changed and still is changing. Activities such as scouting, how-to classes, and recreation fill a busy church's weekly calendar. But perhaps the most significant change is the addition of a weekday program which may be called nursery school, drop-in care, or child care. To illustrate just how widespread weekday programs in churches are, Eileen W. Lindner, Mary C. Mattis, and June R. Rogers have done a monumental study, *When Churches Mind the Children*, of child day care operating in church buildings. They state that "church-housed programs probably constitute the largest group of day care providers in the nation." To understand just what this means in terms of numbers of children, the authors conclude that "it is very likely that the nation's churches collectively house part- or full-day care for several million children." These programs fill a need for both the child and the parent. For the church itself, the message to the community is that the congregation cares about young children and families. It cares enough to provide a nurturing environment for children and education in parenting skills for mothers and fathers.

Good weekday programs that succeed year after year are made up of more than just well-planned rooms and fancy equipment. The director and the board that establish a program are far from finished with their work after they have purchased all the rocking boats, blocks, science equipment, and items for the playground. The fundamental bases for the ongoing success of the program are good relationships between board and director, director and teachers, school staff and parents, and church and school staff. At the heart of these relationships must be a respect for the needs of individuals as well as the needs of groups.

This book will look at these needs in detail, point out areas where conflict is likely to occur, and suggest ways for all concerned to work in harmony with one another.

There is a variety of different weekday programs a church may choose to have. Some of the most common are:

Nursery School

Normally a morning program of two-and-a-half- to three-hours' duration. Activities will include a free-choice time (or "free play"), with the room set up in interest centers. These may include a housekeeping center, blocks and building materials, an art activities center, music, storybooks, science activities, water play, and manipulatives (such as puzzles and small, interlocking building materials for eye-hand coordination). Other activities will include a snack time, outside playground time, and a "circle" or group time for stories, songs, and games. Nursery school programs usually operate two, three, or five mornings a week. Most children who are enrolled are three and four years of age, although some programs include two-year-olds and kindergarten for five-year-olds.

Drop-in Care

Also known as Mothers' Day Out, Parents' Day Out, or Children's Day Out. This kind of program can have several different versions. One type enrolls children for a semester or year at a time. A variation is for the parents to call a day or week in advance and reserve a place. Another form is strictly drop-in; the service is available to anyone who comes by on a first-come basis. Usually drop-in care is for one to two days a week and can be from three to six hours in length. Some programs consist of only infants and toddlers. Other churches also include three- and four-year-olds. Good drop-in care will include age-appropriate activities, interest centers, stories and games, snack time and outside play. It can be a well-planned program as well as baby-sitting.

Child Care

Usually an all-day program. Because child care serves families in which both parents work, the hours of operation can be quite long. Some programs open very early and offer breakfast to the children. Some are in operation until 6:00 or 7:00 P.M. and even provide supper. All day care plans offer a hot lunch. Most programs include infants and children up through four and five years old. Quality child care programs provide a good morning nursery school, lunch, and a more relaxed afternoon including a nap or rest, snack, and outside activities.

Another version of child care is a before- or after-school program for elementary age children which includes a nourishing snack and well-planned age-appropriate games and activities. Some churches even provide a van or bus for the transportation of these children from their schools to the church.

Whatever the program, it should be the very best that a church can provide. It needs to be staffed by well-trained teachers who understand the different stages of development of preschool children. For example, two-and-a-half-year-olds tend to be unbending, unyielding, and ritualistic. A story must always follow juice time, and no pages may be

INTRODUCTION

skipped. Each morning's activities must proceed in the same order that they always have. Two-and-a-half-year-olds like to stay in the same classroom, with the same schedule, day after day. They have trouble making decisions, and teachers of this age group find that children do better with as few choices as possible. The teacher will find that saying, "Today we will have 'Goodnight Moon' for our story," will work better than, "What do you want me to read today?" Since this age group dislikes change, stories must be read again and again. Frances L. Ilg and Louise Bates Ames, in their book *Child Behavior*, say of the two-and-a-half-year-old, "If you read him four stories before bedtime yesterday, he wants four stories—and the same ones, too—today. It is very difficult with many a child of this age to introduce new clothes, new pieces of furniture, new things to eat." New foods at snack time must be brought in one at a time, with long periods elapsing before another new food is presented.

Two-and-a-half-year-olds begin their group experience by being very tentative and investigative in their overtures with other children. A child this age may reach out to touch another child's hair, decide to pull it, then look startled when the other one cries. Pinching another's arm may begin as a harmless, investigative touch. They are also more apt to grab someone else's toy than to ask for it.

Because two-and-a-half-year-olds do not like newness and change, field trips are best saved until they are older. Trips to other parts of the church building, such as the sanctuary or pastor's office, can be difficult for some children and can cause a crying spree. A photographer who arrives to take a group picture may find a very uncooperative class. They also become visibly upset if they see someone in a Santa Claus suit or a clown costume.

Two-and-a-half-year-olds are very interested in their teacher, even while playing. They will engage him or her in conversation, or, if they are on the other side of the room, their eyes will follow the teacher about.

Not all two-and-a-half-year-olds can participate in a group story time. One or two may enjoy sitting quietly and listening while others participate in solitary play activities. Some two-and-a-half-year-olds may not be ready for a group experience. Others enjoy and profit from a few hours away from home. They do best in a very small group, usually of four to six children.

Three-year-olds have lost the antagonistic behavior of two-and-a-half-year-olds. They tend to be gentle and delightful. They find pleasure in each other's company and work happily alongside each other (parallel play) washing dishes and dollies, working puzzles, building roads with blocks, and digging in the sand pile. Sometimes no conversation takes place at all. Because threes love being together, they will frequently all do the same activity. It is not unusual to find the whole class at the art table together or in the block corner together. Most of them are ready for a group experience and can willingly part from their parents for a few hours a day.

Make-believe is more developed in the play of three-year-olds. For example, if a "cake" is made out of wet sand, the child will request that the teacher have a bite. When the teacher pretends also by taking a "bite," the child is delighted.

Ilg and Ames speak of the three-and-a-half-year-old as being in "a period of marked insecurity, disequilibrium, inco-ordination." Teachers do worry about this age group. They fall over objects left on the floor, stumble up the steps, and manage to become twisted in their chairs, sometimes with one or both legs stuck between the rungs. They frequently cover the entire sheet of newsprint when painting or fill up the entire board of play tiles. They use glue and paste generously on paper, sometimes on both sides of it. Some three-and-a-half-year-olds tend to perform poorly on vision and hearing and language screening.

This age child seems insecure and unsure of himself or herself. The teacher will hear complaints such as, "No one will play with me." Teachers of this age group need to offer extra affection and assurance that each child is lovable and worthwhile. Ilg and Ames believe such disequilibrium is normal.

Four-year-olds exhibit an exuberance that is delightful. They seem to have boundless energy, and their curiosity keeps them investigating everything. Their questions are endless. "Why do you have a bandage on your hand? What does your sore look like?" "Are there real people in the TV set?" "Do ladies' heels grow down into their high heels?"

They love to investigate closets, ladies' handbags, containers, clocks, and toilet tanks. They like to see how things work. Because their attention spans are longer than those of three-year-olds, they do not need the close adult supervision that younger children must have.

INTRODUCTION

Social relationships become more important to four-year-olds. They develop special friends, groups of two to four children, and sometimes are so exclusive in their social preferences that other children are ignored.

The artwork of fours begins to look like the objects they say they are drawing. No longer are they scribbling as they did when they were two and three years old. Pictures of people frequently have stick legs and arms coming out of a round head. If the paint they use is thin and drips run down the paper, they will incorporate the drips into the picture by making extra legs on the people or stilts under the house they are drawing.

Children who are four-and-a-half are becoming increasingly independent and are able to stick with projects for long periods of time. Their lengthening attention spans allow teachers to plan for elaborate units that can last for a week and longer. For example, after a trip down the hall to visit the church office, one class of four-and-a-half-year-olds built "office buildings" with their blocks, made office buildings from paper towel cylinders, and made office workers out of clothespins and bits of fabric and yarn. Teachers of the group brought in a typewriter and adding machine, paper punch and notary stamp, and added more play phones and a water cooler. Many new words were added to the children's vocabulary. Interest became keen in storybooks that dealt with mothers and fathers who work in offices. With the teacher's help, the children composed a story about a man who worked in an office and had to use an elevator. This story brought about renewed attention to block building with "elevators." Interest in the office unit lasted three weeks. Later in the year the class asked to hear the story they had made up.

Five-year-olds become interested in school-type activities such as rhyming and asking about individual words in storybooks. If fives have older brothers and sisters in elementary or high school, they like to pretend they are doing homework. Because of their longer attention spans and increased fine motor skills, they are beginning to enjoy working with a large pencil. Some fives are sounding out words on street signs and businesses as they accompany their parents on errands around town. Some are ready to read, and a few fives even teach themselves. However, other five-year-olds may not be ready for formal instruction in reading and should not be pushed into a reading program. Play is still the most important avenue of learning, and classrooms for this age group should contain well-planned interest centers. The morning's activities for fives should include plenty of time for them to participate in free-choice activities.

As a group, preschool children are very literal and believe everything an adult says. For example, Ned, a three-year-old, climbed on his teacher's lap several times one morning, and each time pulled down her chin and peered inside her mouth. During one of these investigations he asked, "Jesus, are you down there?" The teacher told Ned's mother about the incident when she came to take him home. She thought for a long time, then remembered, "Oh, I told him yesterday that Jesus lives inside us!"

INTRODUCTION

Because young children are so literal, they will occasionally be quite terrified of fairy tales and other stories that contain violent incidents, such as a wolf eating a grandmother or a witch imprisoning children. Some others may be visibly upset. Such stories are better saved for middle childhood.

Young children are not yet ready for abstract concepts. Some Bible stories may be beyond their grasp because they contain words such as *courage, blessing, heir, mystery, offering,* and *praise.* The list could become very lengthy. Good teachers are able to rephrase stories so that they are stated in concrete terms and can then be better understood by preschoolers.

Play is the business of childhood. Through play, children learn about their world. They may engage in role-playing or dramatic play, for example, and act out what it would be like to be a father, mother, gas station attendant, mail carrier, cashier at the grocery, or character on television. Imagination and fantasy are a part of play.

Play helps children become active discoverers of the world and develop strategies for problem solving. They pour water or sand back and forth from one container to another watching how much each container will hold. They roll small cars down an incline, then put a block on the incline to see if it will roll down too. They build doorways with blocks, then see what will fit through the openings. They stack blocks again and again to see how they balance and how high the stack can be made before it falls.

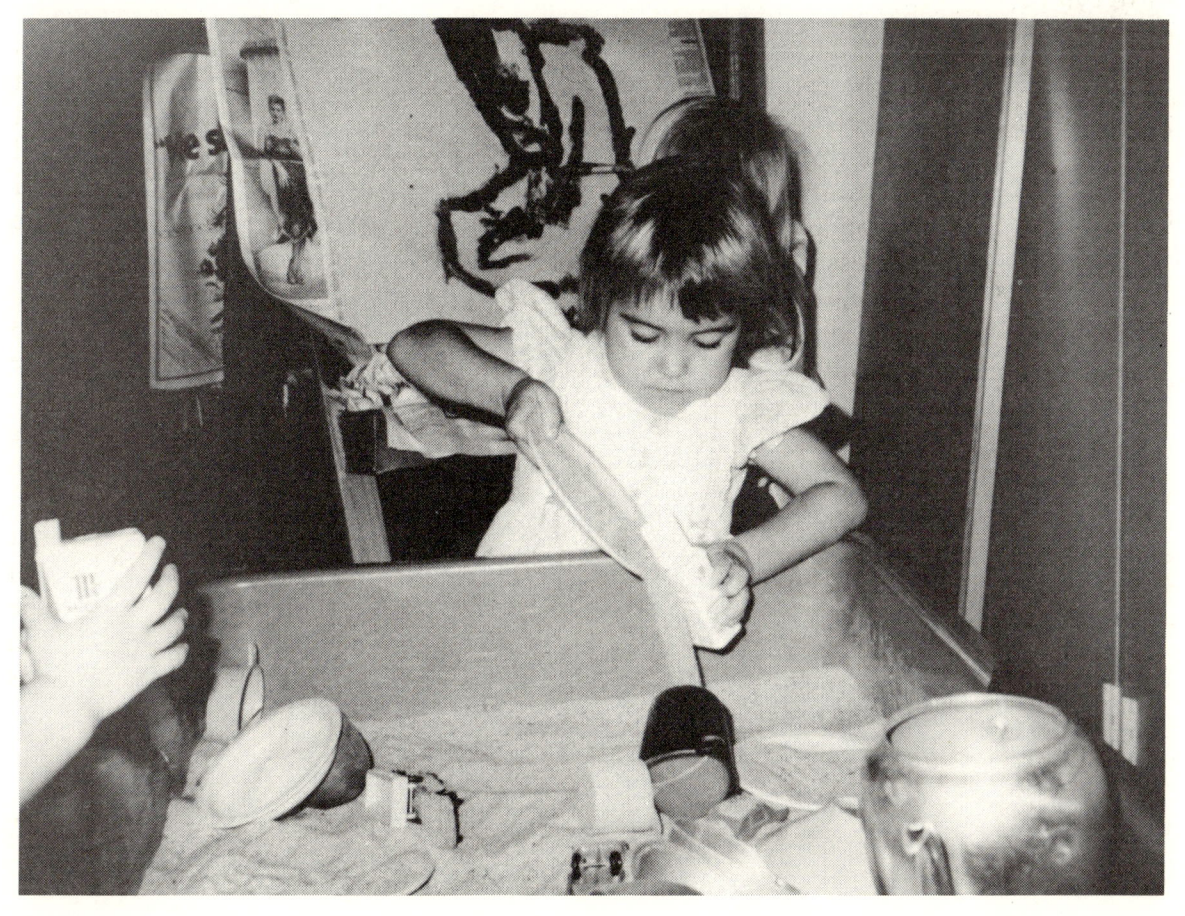

It is during play that teachers have their greatest opportunity. They can suggest different strategies to increase learning.

—"What do you think will happen if you put a block under the incline?"

—"Will the Legos roll down like the car does?"

—"Will this bottle hold that much water or will you need a bigger bottle?"

—"Will the rubber horse fit through the opening or is it too tall?"

Such questions stimulate children's thinking and help them open up their world by considering more possibilities.

Teachers encourage children with social relationships during play. For example, a group may shun a child by announcing, "No, you can't play with us!" The teacher can show the child a strategy for entering a group by suggesting, "Perhaps Laura can deliver mail to your house. What can we use for letters?"

Teachers can be role models in Christian living. Faith easily manifests itself when a teacher working with children makes comments such as:

—"We won't mind staying indoors today. God planned for the rain to give our flowers and grass some water."

—"Thank you, God, for Jamie's new tooth."

Teachers can help children develop moral values during play with well-phrased and well-timed comments such as:

—"It's okay to have curly hair. Each one of us is different."

—"We have only three crackers left in the basket. How can we divide them so everyone will have some?"

—"It hurts Tommy to be pushed off the trike, and I can't let you do that. This is his turn now. You will be next."

These strategies, or techniques of teaching that good teachers use, optimize learning for young children. The preschool years represent a time when learning is swift and curiosity is at a peak. Indeed, the preschool years are perhaps the most significant in the development of children. Well-trained teachers are essential. A church that makes a commitment for a weekday program must also make a commitment for an excellent program.

CONSIDERING A WEEKDAY PROGRAM

A few mothers in a congregation may provide the original impetus for a preschool. They might comment when they meet for circle groups or around the coffeepot on Sunday morning that they need a nursery school. The remarks may be prompted by a desire to get out of the house occasionally or by a wish to find some friends for their children or by some perceived need for help with pre-reading skills. However, providing a program based on the needs of a few mothers will not be enough. For a weekday program to succeed year after year, it must be based on a real need both in the church and in the community.

A church that has many young mothers and fathers in its congregation has a nucleus of interest and talent for a preschool to develop from an idea into reality. Knowing that it is their own children who will benefit, these parents will become the committee members, the playground builders, the buyers of supplies and equipment, and in some instances, the staff of the school itself.

A church program that looks inward and provides only for its own members becomes static and usually ceases altogether as the congregation grows more gray-haired. An older congregation moves on to other interests and places its emphasis elsewhere, such as on programs for teens or senior citizens, support groups, or food and fellowship for nursing home residents.

Reaching out into the community becomes a way of filling the school. A church that opens its doors to families outside the congregation shows it cares about children regardless of their church affiliation or lack of it. It simply wants to provide a good program for children, no matter who they are.

Congregations sometimes hope that the addition of a weekday program will bring a lot of new families into the church's membership. It is true that some will join. A weekday program that serves the community will include families who are unchurched. However, increasing church attendance should not be the main reason for offering a weekday program. Programs for young children are an outreach and a ministry to the community and are a response to the needs of people.

Lyle Schaller, in his book *Effective Church Planning*, says:

THE CHURCH-RELATED PRESCHOOL

> Identifying... the potentialities in ministry tend[s] to cause people to look to the future, to be conscious of the assets and strengths of the congregation... to see these as foundation stones or building blocks for expanding the outreach of the church, to recognize new possibilities for ministry.... The potentialities-based approach tends to raise the level of congregational self-esteem.

Congregations want to reach out to others. It is good for those of us who are contemplating a weekday program or who already have one to show our congregations how it can be a ministry. By doing so we help church members build self-esteem by knowing they are meeting a very real need. A program for young children helps a congregation reach out to the community and be of service to it. Let us look at some of the ways a weekday program is a ministry.

1. We are role models in Christian living for young children and their families. We accept all people, no matter who they are or whether they belong to another church or religion. It is unconditional acceptance. We give them our love, care, and concern.
2. We offer a program in quality education for young children without a profit-making motive behind it. This frees us to maintain a good pupil-teacher ratio. It allow us to buy good equipment and enables us to help provide expenses for teacher training that allows our teachers to become better at their profession.
3. We offer programs and study groups for parents of children in the weekday program that offer help with parenting skills as well as opportunities for fun and fellowship within the circle of the church family. We welcome our weekday families when they join us for worship or when they participate in our other outreach programs, such as collecting food and clothing for the poor.
4. We reach out to our weekday families during their times of need such as illness or death in the family, divorce, problems with alcohol or drug abuse, or loss of a job.

Use this list to stimulate your thinking about other ways your weekday program can be a ministry in your community. Add your ideas to the above list.

For any church contemplating a weekday program, it is necessary to determine just how great a need exists through a survey of the congregation and of the neighborhood. Church records should be studied to determine how many actual preschoolers there are. A survey of the surrounding community will show whether the area contains many young families with children under five. One church placed posters in stores and shops near the church (the grocery, dry cleaners, and clothing stores) asking, "How can our church meet the needs of this community?" Pencils and paper and a shoe box for answers were provided. Although some church members had thought that no one would take the time to answer and no ideas would appear in the shoe box, they were surprised that people did respond. Some answers requested more activities for teens. One person even felt the church should provide a community swimming pool. But the response that appeared over and over again was that a nursery school was needed, even though there were already two large church preschools close by.

Other ways to survey the need for a preschool in the community is to check with women's clubs, analyze school census records, and talk with real estate companies and school officials. Population density, average age of the population, number of one-parent households, housing trends, and projected school enrollments will be of interest.

Hearsay alone can result either in programs that are not filled or in the wrong kind of program for a church. It cannot be assumed, for example, that a nursery school program

CONSIDERING A WEEKDAY PROGRAM

would be the best choice if many one-parent families are in the community, nor would day care meet the needs if most mothers do not work. Other preschools in the area will share whether or not they are usually full and have a waiting list, or if they struggle every year to fill classes.

Surveys are important because they will present a fairly accurate picture of the needs in your community and your church. When you undertake a survey, you will be looking for some of the following information:
1. How does the congregation feel about sharing its classrooms with children who may not be children of church members?
2. Is the church willing or able to appropriate any money for equipment or for scholarships?
3. Does the church have a pool of talent for teachers and substitutes?
4. How accepting will the congregation be of the weekday program?
5. Does the community around the church have families who are interested in participating in the program?
6. What are the specific needs of these families? What age group of children will participate?

In order to have a grasp of your congregation's thinking about a weekday program, a church survey could be included with the church's Sunday bulletin or tucked inside the newsletter.

You will also be interested in determining whether your community has a need for a weekday program for young children. A survey form could be passed out or mailed to homes in the immediate neighborhood.

You will find that people will respond to surveys if they are kept as short as possible and if there is a convenient way to return them. Including a stamped envelope with the survey will enable you to get back a greater return, although some money must be spent in order to do so. Check with your local post office about obtaining special rates for bulk mailings.

Some surveys can be made by placing eye-appealing posters and survey sheets in local businesses where young families shop regularly.

See the samples of survey forms on pages 22 and 23 for ideas as you create your own forms.

Even after a church preschool has been in existence for some time, a reexamination of the need for it is important. Church needs as well as community needs can change. If the surrounding area contains mothers who are starting back to work because families now need two paychecks, then it may be necessary to add day care to the existing half-day program. Or it may be desirable to shift to after-school care if your community's children are now older. There may be mothers who need to be away for appointments or volunteer work or just to have a few hours to themselves to keep from climbing the walls. These families will want drop-in care.

The neighborhood around a church can change with the passage of time, becoming less densely populated with families with young children. Some churches grow very large within a few years and add so many morning programs for adults that baby-sitting for those who attend may be more necessary than a preschool.

This reappraisal of needs can be done when a new pastor comes to the church or when new board or committee members replace old members who have rotated off.

Sample

CHURCH SURVEY

Our church has received many requests for a weekday program for young children. A study committee is being appointed to look into the feasibility of such a program. We would appreciate your views. Please share with us the following information.

1. Do you feel that having a program for young children in several of the Sunday school classrooms during the week would be good stewardship of our building? These rooms normally sit idle during the week.

    _____ Yes   _____ No

2. Which of the following programs would you and your children use? Please check.

    _____ Child Care
    _____ Nursery School
    _____ Drop-in Care
    _____ After-school Care

3. Would you be interested in helping by

    _____ Being on the planning committee?
    _____ Teaching in the weekday program?
    _____ Substituting when needed?

                                                    Study Committee

Name _____

Address _____

Sample

NEIGHBORHOOD SURVEY

Dear Neighbor,

Your community church [insert the name of your church] has appointed a study committee to look into the possibility of developing a weekday program for young children. We are making a survey to determine whether a need exists in our community for such a program. Please take a few minutes to answer the following questions. A stamped envelope is enclosed for your response.

1. Do you have children who would participate in a church-sponsored program for young children?

    _____ Yes   _____ No

2. If so, which program would best suit your needs?

    _____ Child Care
    _____ Nursery School
    _____ Drop-in Care
    _____ After-school Care

3. Please list the ages of your children.

4. If our survey indicates a need exists and a weekday program is established, would you like to have further information about it? If so, please share your name and address.

Name _____

Address _____

You may also call our church office [phone number of church], for information about our weekday program.
We appreciate your help.

Study Committee

THE CHURCH-RELATED PRESCHOOL

Reassessment of the church's needs as well as community needs assures the church that it is responding with the kind of weekday program that is appropriate. It is good for any institution to examine itself. Some questions that should be considered are:
1. Why do we have a weekday program?
2. Do we still need for the church to help financially or can we now pay for some of the janitorial work or the utilities?
3. Is the weekday program still a part of the church program?
4. Is the weekday program still meeting a need in the community?

Congregations are sometimes asked to rent space to a group wishing to start a school or to an already established school looking for a new home. Renting space to such a group might cause problems if your church and the school have no common goals. What may initially seem like a good idea can turn out to be a difficult situation unless both the school and the church make an extra effort. Because it is hard to share space with others who are not part of the church family, resentment may build up. Communication between the two groups will not be easy. A "we/they" attitude could develop even under the best of conditions. "They used all our newsprint"; "They always leave the rooms so messy!" This lack of a sense of sharing or a sense of community occurs when groups are unrelated. It is easy to blame someone with whom you have never worked, or never shared a family night supper.

Renting to a school takes away all the work and effort of starting one and allows space to be used that would normally be idle during the week. For a rental program to be a success, good and frequent communication between the two groups is a must. The more we get to know people as persons, the better we can accept them. Planned meetings between the Sunday school teachers and the weekday teachers are a necessity in the fall before school opens and several times during the school year. If these meetings can be social as well as business discussions about supplies and room use, each group will more easily accept the problems with which the others must work. Coffee and dessert will help.

It is also necessary for school administrators and church staff to stay in close communication and to acquaint each other with their goals and how they plan to accomplish them. The school may need scholarships, and the church could provide them as part of its benevolence giving. Or the church may appreciate having literature sent home to the children's parents about the church's Sunday schedule and evening activities.

When the rent charged a school yields more money for a church than it needs to cover the expense of having the school, the church must seriously consider the question of whether it should be in the business of making a profit. After the extra time the janitor puts in is given a dollar value, portions of the utility bills are assigned, and money is set aside for maintenance, the church does not need to collect beyond these amounts. Charging more than a church needs to cover operating costs may jeopardize its tax-exempt status.

Another factor to consider is that when a church rents space to outsiders for a school, it is, in effect, giving up its birthright. The congregation loses its chance to have its philosophy of education and ministry reflected in the school. Renting to an outside group may make sense to a church, however, if the community need is clearly there and yet its members are so busy and involved with numerous other church-related endeavors that its talent and work pool are stretched to the limit.

If renting space is an avenue that your church wants to pursue, all possible problems associated with it must be dealt with before a lease is signed. It is always better to anticipate a difficulty and work out its solution beforehand. Let us look at some possible problems and solutions.

Problems That Could Occur

1. There are too many children for the number of teachers.

2. Educational standards are different from the church's standards.

3. The school does not take good care of church property.

4. The school is too exclusive in admitting children.

Solutions Worked Out Beforehand

1. Schools that overcrowd usually do so because they want to make more money. Insist ahead of time what the pupil-teacher ratio will be.

2. Allow a school to rent your building only if the quality of its program is a good match with the church's standards. Some schools are intent on pushing young children into an academic program that is too demanding.

3. Draw up a lease agreement which states that the school will paint the rooms it rents every two years and will keep all shared equipment in good repair.

4. Insist that children are admitted regardless of their ethnic, cultural, or religious background.

Churches that are considering renting space to outsiders must also look at their own insurance program carefully to see if the liability is affected.

A one-year renewable lease is better than a long-term lease because it allows the church to reevaluate the school each year.

THE WEEKDAY PROGRAM— A PART OF THE CHURCH

Regardless of whether there is a community need for a weekday program or whether the church itself has enough young families with preschoolers, the congregation also must want the school. Sunday school teachers should be willing to share their rooms with weekday teachers, giving up precious closet space, taking down bulletin board posters after class is over, and putting them back up again the next week. Floors and bathrooms will require more attention from the custodian. Electric bills and heating costs may increase slightly. Parents of preschoolers will use parking spaces in the parking lot. A playground will have to be built, sometimes usurping beautiful shrubbery and flower beds, and a fence will have to be erected.

Sometimes members of a congregation may initially believe a weekday program for young children will be a good use of their building without taking a long, hard look at the problems associated with having the program. Churches can philosophically accept Christ's directive to let the little children come. Yet when they do come they frequently have dirty hands and manage to get fingerprints on classroom walls and windows. It is analogous to a young couple who decide they want a child without thinking about the strain on the family budget, the demands on their time, and the arrangement of the home's furnishings that go hand in hand with all the joys of parenthood.

Even when everyone is in agreement that having a weekday program is good stewardship of space, in reality it is difficult for groups to share ownership of space. Although the rooms belong to the church, the people who actually paint them, make curtains for the windows, find interesting pictures for the walls, and drag in the bookcases are the ones who will feel the strongest about ownership of the rooms. When two groups use a room, the ones who have invested more time and energy will feel the strongest sense of ownership. Some ministers feel that the sharing of space is a major problem, especially in churches where almost all rooms have joint use. One church's classrooms, for example, have taken on the appearance of school classrooms, and all storage is used by the weekday teachers. Sunday school teachers must carry in their supplies in baskets. Such a situation does not promote good feelings.

Joint usage requires careful planning. Some ideas that work are:

THE WEEKDAY PROGRAM—A PART OF THE CHURCH

1. A high-school student who wants to earn extra money can be hired to move small tables and chairs out of a classroom on Friday afternoons and bring in adult-size furniture. On Sunday afternoons, the furniture can be moved back. Many teenagers want part-time work. This task could also be done by the custodian.
2. Reversible bulletin boards can be made so that each group does not have to put its pictures and posters away, but can simply turn the bulletin boards around each Friday and Sunday.
3. Each group can share equally the storage space as well as equipment and supplies. Some weekday directors keep a closet stocked with paper, paint, and glue for the Sunday teachers as well as for the weekday teachers. The directors of Christian education at other churches order for both the Sunday school and the weekday program. Manipulatives, games, records, musical instruments, and other pieces of equipment are used jointly. Items are then thought of as "ours."
4. Some churches have found that a weekday program is best held in the same classrooms that are used for very young children on Sunday mornings. This may limit the size of the preschool, but the amount of time spent moving furniture to prepare for each group is considerably less.
5. Frequent meetings are held between Sunday school teachers and weekday teachers who share rooms. Good communication is a necessity. It is far better for people to work out problems face-to-face than to complain about them in other church group meetings.

In addition to problems of sharing space, congregations need to view the weekday program as a part of the church's total plan. For the weekday program to exist in harmony with all the other programs of the church, it must keep before the congregation how it is meeting a need in the community and how it is a ministry. Items in the church newsletter and the Sunday bulletin may, for example, inform the congregation about how the children and parents of the school responded to a request for baby clothes for needy families. Or, some of the children's remarks as they prepare for Thanksgiving and Christmas can be quoted. A news item that appeared in one church newspaper told of a little girl watching water as it boiled before fresh cranberries were added. "Look! The water is jumping up and down!" Such news items capture the fun and excitement associated with working with children and make the readers glad the school is a part of the total program of the church.

Another church weekday program always has posters outside each classroom door announcing the units of study. "God Plans for Autumn" was the title for one such poster which displayed the children's art. This poster told parents and church members alike that the weekday curriculum related to the Sunday program.

Some churches and their weekday preschools exist for years in a kind of deadlock situation, each tolerating the other, because care has not been taken to establish the school as an integral part of the church program. Even though the weekday program is set up to be governed by a church committee and, hence, is part of the church structure, the congregation must also view the weekday program as its own.

Although there will always be a portion of a congregation that will resent sharing the church with families who are nonmembers, the success of the weekday program will depend upon good communication. When information is regularly channeled into the congregation about how the weekday program is meeting a need in the community and how it is a viable ministry and an outreach to the community, then such a congregation will usually be more willing to undergo the changes necessary to accommodate a program for young children.

Congregations can open their doors to children and parents more easily when they see that the weekday families are experiencing acceptance, love, and forgiveness as they are involved in a week-long program, not just a Sunday morning one. It is Christianity in action when others are invited into the church's fellowship and care.

Congregations will also be more accepting of weekday programs when they understand that families have always looked to the church for the moral development of their children. Parents who do not go to church themselves often know the value of having Christian teachers. Some mothers and fathers feel they cannot quite do the job of imparting faith and look to the church for help. The weekday program that is available to everyone, not just members' children, is meeting parents' needs for moral and spiritual help with their families.

Congregations are also more apt to view the weekday program as an integral part of the church when they have an opportunity to learn that the policy-making committee or board of the school is a church committee or subcommittee, and that teachers in the weekday and Sunday programs work together. In fact, the same teachers often teach in both.

SETTING UP AN ADMINISTRATIVE BOARD

Once a church decides that it wants a weekday program, setting up the board or committee to administer it becomes its next priority. Any interested group or even the minister can bring before the governing body of the church the suggestion to appoint a committee or board that will develop the program.

The governing body of the church can ensure that a board become a part of the church structure. It can be a separate committee along with all the other church committees, or it can be a subcommittee under the Christian education department.

Sometimes the planning committee that conducted the surveys and looked into the feasibility of having a weekday program becomes a part of the first board. Once a board is a reality, new members can be added to the original group.

Someone with a background in education—particularly early childhood education or child development—will be an invaluable member, as will someone with expertise in business and finance. Persons who have worked in public relations or in personnel will be helpful. A church staff member, such as the director of Christian education or one of the ministers, will keep before the committee the goals of the church. Parents from the school and members of the congregation who are interested in the welfare of young children will make significant contributions. And the director of the school will be a member.

The membership of the board should rotate so there are no more than one-third new people on the committee during any one year. After the school is under way, two- or three-year terms are better than a one-year term. New members go through a learning process in familiarizing themselves with the school and are more helpful after they have been members for a while.

It is important for the board to decide what its areas of responsibility are and to define those areas in its bylaws or guidelines. These will be clearly different from the areas of responsibility of the director.

Functions of the Board

1. To develop policy for the school
2. To develop a workable budget

3. To report periodically to the governing body of the church and to the congregation
4. To develop a plan for evaluating the school staff, the budget, the kinds of families applying and their needs, and the board itself
5. To hire a director and staff
6. To approve personnel selected by the director
7. To provide training for new members of the board
8. To do public relations, function as liaison between the school and the church, and interpret the work of the school to the church
9. To support the director and the staff

GOAL SETTING

After the board is officially established, its first task will be that of goal setting. Let us look at the goal-setting process in relation to starting the weekday program.

Step 1: Identifying Needs

Analyzing all the data from the church and community surveys will give a fairly accurate picture of the type of program that your church will want to offer. You will be able to pinpoint the need from the surveys and determine whether a child care or a nursery school program is more appropriate for you to develop.

Step 2: Plotting Strategy

This next step involves determining how the need will be met. Ask yourself the following questions:
1. Will the weekday program use the rooms that are used for three- and four-year-olds on Sunday?
2. Can other classrooms also be used?
3. Can the church afford to give a sum of money for the equipment and supplies needed to get started?
4. How will people be informed that the church is starting a weekday program?
5. Can another church committee help with scholarships?

A preliminary budget can be drawn up at this time to give the board members a picture of how the program will fare financially.

Step 3: Determining Long-Term and Short-Term Goals

Your short-term goal might be to start with only one or two classes of children. However, you may feel that the need in the community is great enough that the church will want to expand the program as quickly as possible and add other classes the following year.

Step 4: Setting Specific Objectives

1. *How* will you pay for start-up costs? Will registration fees cover supplies and equipment? Can you charge enough tuition to make the school self-supporting? Do you need to be licensed?

SETTING UP AN ADMINISTRATIVE BOARD

2. *Where* will the playground be located? Where will storage be? Is there a place for a school office?
3. *When* will a director be hired? When will the school open? When will you accept applications from families?
4. *Who* will take care of advertising? Who will draw up a job description for the director's job? Who will contact the state and local licensing offices?

Step 5: Acting

Once a board has reached this step, the weekday program is well on its way to becoming a reality. Each member of the board will have assignments to complete by a certain date. A director will have been hired who will be interviewing teacher applicants. The board will have the final approval on the staff of the program. Licensing will be under way.

Step 6: Evaluating

1. Is the program adequately staffed?
2. Is the equipment you have been able to accumulate adequate?
3. Is there a safe indoor and outdoor environment for young children?
4. Are you charging enough tuition to adequately meet your needs?
5. Are the lines of communication open between the Sunday teachers and the weekday teachers so that sharing space is easy?

DETERMINING POLICIES

Policy making is one of the main functions of a board. What is policy? It is simply a course of action or conduct, or a set of rules, under which the program operates. It is the job of the preschool board to draw up a set of bylaws or guidelines that clearly state for everyone involved just what policy exists for the school. That policy centers around these main areas:

1. The Purpose of the School

Why does the school exist? What will the name of the school be? Who will sponsor the school?

2. Personnel Policy

The board or committee decides how much education the director and the teachers must have.

Should teachers be required to have a college degree? Should their college major be in child development or early childhood education, or will a related major suffice? How much experience should teachers have? One year, or more? (For a sample teacher's job description see the chapter entitled "Teachers.")

For the director, will an undergraduate degree be sufficient, or will an advanced degree be necessary? What kind of administrative skills shall the director have? (See the chapter entitled "The Director" for a sample job description.)

Other issues that the board or committee must decide on when writing a personnel policy are the following:
a. How much sick leave will be allowed?
b. Will the school underwrite the cost of substitutes?
c. How much will be deducted from a teacher's salary if an illness goes beyond a week or two?
d. What other benefits will the school provide for the staff? (Hospitalization and retirement benefits are possibilities.)

It should be stated, also, that school staff are to report to the director and that the director reports to the board or committee. Precisely defining the process of accountability prevents future problems. At no time should a board allow a teacher to come directly to it with a problem or grievance. The teacher should first talk with the director. If the conflict is such that the director cannot resolve it, the director should bring it to the board for help.

3. *Financial Policy and Budget*

The board states how it will receive income. The main source will be through tuition, although some money may come from scholarships, from fund raisers, or from church funds. The board decides what percent of its income will be funneled into each expense category. This budget-making process usually allocates approximately 80 percent to 85 percent for staff salaries, its biggest expense. A smaller quantity, approximately 12 percent to 14 percent, goes for equipment and supplies. Remaining monies are used for meetings, professional growth and educational development of staff, insurance (if it is not part of the church's insurance policy), and telephone. A contingency fund covers unexpected needs, uncollected tuition, and less than capacity enrollment. If the church does not underwrite the utilities and janitorial help, then provision must be made for these items in the budget. Some programs pay rent or a fee for building use. Tuition must be made higher if these three expenses have to be paid by the preschool, in order to still provide a quality environment for young children and adequate salaries for staff. (For another discussion of budget items in terms of percentages, we refer the reader to Clare Cherry, Barbara Harkness, and Kay Kuzma, *Nursery School Management Guide*, Fearon, Calif.: Lear Seigler, Inc., 1973.)

Some church preschools have a separate budget and a separate bank account. Others choose to include their income and expenses as part of the overall church budget. There are advantages and disadvantages to each method.

An advantage in having a separate budget and bank account for the school's income is that the board decides how it will be spent, allocating certain portions to each expense category.

A disadvantage in using a separate budget and bank account is that the church will not have direct access to the budget and may assume that the preschool generates a lot of income and, therefore, does not need any help from the church. This disadvantage can be offset by always providing the governing body of the church with a copy of the budget and minutes of the board's meetings, particularly those that deal with monetary decisions such as the purchase of equipment and teachers' salaries.

SETTING UP AN ADMINISTRATIVE BOARD

The advantage in having school money deposited in the church account is that it helps the church realize that the school is a part of its overall program and ministry. The disadvantage may occur when church funds become low and the potential exists for school funds also becoming low. This disadvantage can be offset by earmarking all money for the school's needed expenses and setting aside a contingency fund for unexpected needs.

Sample Budget Line Items

Income	Registration
	Tuition
Expenses	Salaries
	Substitutes
	Consumable supplies (paint, paper, glue)
	Indoor equipment
	Playground equipment
	Snacks (juice, crackers, cups, napkins)
	Workers' compensation
	FICA tax
	Professional training
	Meetings
	Car allowance
	Petty cash
	Miscellaneous
	Contingency
	If Necessary:
	Phone
	Utilities
	Rent
	Janitor

4. Enrollment Policy

The board will decide the order of preference by which children will be admitted into the school. Many churches choose to admit members' children first. Next in order will come children who were enrolled in the school the previous year, providing the school has been in existence. Third in order will be children of new families. These are taken on a first-come basis according to the dates on the applications.

Classes may also be filled according to the boy-girl ratio, allotting half the spaces for each.

The class size will be determined in the enrollment policy. The board will determine how many square feet of space exist in each classroom and decide how many children each room can handle (at thirty-five square feet per child). Very young children thrive best in small groups (fewer than eighteen) with two to three teachers per group. Too many children in one large classroom can be difficult to work with, even if the pupil-teacher ratio is right.

Part of the enrollment policy will be a determination of the age groups the weekday program will serve. Will the school begin with three-year-olds or twos? By age three, most children will enjoy and profit from being in a small group for a few hours each day. A preschool experience adds a new dimension to a child's life, such as the opportunity to get along with others his or her own age, develop friendships, and enjoy learning activities that some homes cannot provide. There will even be some two-year-olds who are ready for a small group. Their readiness is determined by their willingness to be away from their parents for a few hours.

Will the preschool include only four-year-olds or will there be a kindergarten for the fives? If there will be a kindergarten, can provisions be made for a prekindergarten as an in-between step for some children? Will there be a cutoff birth date for each of the classes, or will the director be free to place the children according to the developmental level of each child? Some three-year-olds who are developmentally four need to be with an older group. Some fours are still only three developmentally and need to be with a younger group.

Occasionally private schools such as church schools are asked by parents to accept a child in kindergarten who is not fully five years old. In addition to making the decision based on the child's developmental readiness for kindergarten, consideration must also be given to the time after the current school year when the family will be looking for a first grade for the child. Almost all public schools have a cutoff date for first grade, and, depending on the state in which the family resides, the date can range from August 15 to January 31. Enrolling an underage child in kindergarten can cause a difficulty for the family the following year unless the church or another private school has first-grade openings that will be available.

5. Tuition Policy

The board determines when tuition is due—weekly, monthly, or by the semester or year. From an analysis of the program's budget, the amount of tuition can be set. Will the last month's tuition of the school year be required along with September's payment? Will it be due by the first of the month or the tenth?

Registration fees can be another source of income for the weekday program. Some churches use these fees for equipment and supplies; others add the amount to their expected income and it becomes a part of the working budget. Still others apply part of the registration fee toward the tuition due from each family.

There will always be families who move away during the school year. The board or committee will want to set a policy for prorating tuition for the portion of the month that the child attends school. Since it is unrealistic to expect a family to pay tuition for the time after a child is withdrawn, school budgets should reflect a less than maximum enrollment. Sometimes another child can be taken from a waiting list. It may also happen that the place will never be filled for the rest of the school year.

Occasionally a family may be asked to withdraw a child from the school for health reasons or an emotional problem. Again, tuition can be prorated for the amount of time the child has attended.

6. Scholarship Policy

It may be quite natural for a board to plan for scholarships if the school serves an area that is not affluent. However, even in affluent areas marriages break up, and mothers go back to work and need help. Some families may be caught in a web of debt for medical expenses or support of in-laws. A scholarship policy is a necessity for each school. A sample of a scholarship application is on the next page.

The board's first step is to decide who is eligible. Listed below are some considerations.
  a. Families who are at or below federal guidelines for poverty level may need tuition help.
  b. Ministers' children, the weekday teachers' children, or children of other church staff may be in need of partial scholarships.
  c. Some rebate, perhaps 5 percent or 10 percent of tuition, may be appropriate for church members' children.

Because people tend to appreciate something more if it is not free, a small charge for all families on scholarships may be the wisest course.

7. *Health Policy*

To protect the health and well-being of the whole school, the board will need to set standards for inoculations for childhood diseases that will be required before a child can enter school. A child receives a series of three diphtheria-tetanus-whooping cough inoculations during the first year of life, and a booster is given when the child is ready for preschool. Polio, measles, mumps, and rubella inoculations are necessary, as is a skin test for tuberculosis. Preschool and day care centers in large urban areas will find that occasionally children do have a positive TB test and need to be under a doctor's care. School will have to be delayed for these children until they are free of disease.

Some states have strict licensing standards for preschools and day care centers, and the board will need to adopt these standards as part of the health policy. However, board members will also have to deal with whether they will accept non-inoculated children of families whose religions prohibit it. Since churches' preschools and day care centers are private rather than public, this decision has to be an individual one. See page 37 for a sample of a health form.

8. *Curriculum Policy*

Boards do not plan every song and story used in the preschool. This is the classroom teacher's prerogative because the teacher is the one who is tuned into the needs, the developmental level, and the interests of the children. These may be different with each group. The director's job includes making sure that goal- and age-appropriate activities are used. Difficulties may arise when a board assumes its function is to plan curriculum. Most board members do not have the background or training for such a task; directors and teachers do. It is, however, part of the board's function to prescribe that the curriculum of the weekday program be based on two criteria:
  a. That the curriculum focus on a basic Christian orientation
  b. That the curriculum materials be compatible with the Sunday school curriculum

It can be very unsettling for a congregation to learn that its weekday program is using curriculum materials that are not compatible with the curriculum used on Sunday. Problems can be avoided from the start if the preschool or center understands and supports the goals, objectives, and theology of the Sunday school program by using a curriculum complementary to these ideas.

Sample

SCHOLARSHIP APPLICATION

All information is strictly confidential and will not be given to any individual or group other than the committee directly concerned with granting financial aid for the school.

Funds for financial aid come from a portion of the school's income, from gifts, from benevolence funds of the church, and from occasional special gifts. Since such funds are limited, we will grant them to those whose need is most acute.

1. Child's name _____ Birth date _____
2. Address _____ Phone _____
3. Class for which applying _____
4. Father's name and address _____
   _____
5. Mother's name and address _____
   _____
6. Person financially responsible for tuition
   _____
7. Please list other dependent children.

Name of Child	Age	School	Tuition

8. List any other dependents and the amount of financial assistance you are responsible for.
   _____
   _____
   _____

9. Please list your monthly financial obligations.
   _____
   _____
   _____
   _____

10. Father's occupation and income
    _____

11. Mother's occupation and income
    _____

12. Please list the make and year of your car(s).
    _____

                          Signed _____

Sample

MEDICAL FORM

Child's name_____ Birth date_____

Is child under regular care of a doctor?_____

Why? _____

Is child on any regular medication? _____

If so, what? _____

Has child had any communicable disease? _____

What? _____ When? _____

General health _____

Eyes _____

Ears _____

Has child any history of convulsions? _____

Is child subject to any dietary regulations? _____

If yes, what are they? _____

Has child had any major surgery? _____

Does child have any physical reason for not participating in normal school activities such as outdoor play?
_____
_____

Does child have allergies? _____

Immunization Record

	Date 1st dose	Date 2nd dose	Date 3rd dose	Date 1st booster	Date 2nd booster

DPT _____

Polio _____

Measles Vaccine—
Rubeola _____

Mumps _____

Rubella Vaccine _____

Tuberculosis test
(Tine skin test) Date_____ Reaction _____

   Physician's signature _____

     Date _____

9. Policy on the Makeup of the Board

Once a board for the weekday program has been established by the governing body of the church, the original members decide who will be on the board with them. Shall it be made up only of church members or shall some parents from the school also have a place? Will someone serve from the community at large, bringing some area of expertise that the congregation may lack? For example, a pediatrician or attorney may be an important addition, but neither might be found on the church rolls. What about an architect or builder? Such persons may be willing to serve on the board for a year, or even for a shorter time in an advisory capacity. The policy-making tasks of the board will include making provisions for helpful assistance when it is needed.

A board that completely changes every year can never have the continuity that is necessary for a good understanding of the preschool. Such turnover means that new members must start from scratch, learning about the philosophy and operation of the preschool. Only after this indoctrination period is over do board members become helpful and contributing. A board will want to devise a means of rotation so that no more than one-third new members are brought to it in any one year and most members are serving two- or three-year terms.

The board decides how much representation it will have from the congregation at large and how much from the governing body of the church. A representative from the church staff, such as the minister or director of Christian education, also is needed on the board. A church staff member is usually ex-officio (the position is without voting rights). Not only is input from the church staff valuable to the preschool, but this person will be able to interpret the value of the school to the total ministry of the church.

10. Policy on Ministry to Families

Families of the preschool's children will not all be church members. Some may belong to other churches, some may attend a church irregularly, and some may have no contact with a church other than bringing their children to the preschool. Because the responsibility of Christians is to minister to everyone, not just member families, the board will want to define ways in which the church, and more specifically, the preschool can reach out to the children's parents. The purpose is not simply to gather in new members for the church (although this will happen with some families) but to meet needs for all parents. Parents' needs center around two main areas:

a. The need for more parenting education

All parents want to do a good job of parenting. More often than not, parents are miles away from grandparents and other family members who could give help readily when problems arise about raising children. They all remember their own parents' methods of discipline—even the very phrasing that was used, the tone of voice, and the look on their faces. They know that some old techniques worked and some did not. Very few persons have taken courses in high school or college that would prepare them for such an important role as parenting. Parents want skills that are effective. When a preschool or day care board develops policy for a planned program of offering help with parenting skills, it is meeting a real need. That policy may state that there will be several parent meetings during the year, or a workshop of several weeks' duration. The director will be aware of the subject matter that will be most helpful to parents. Depending on needs and interests, the program may cover nutrition, family safety, spotting learning disabilities, discipline, autonomy, building self-esteem, and developing a good emotional climate in the home. The board may present these opportunities for those who wish to participate, or, if the need is acute, it may decide to make the meetings mandatory and to make attendance a condition for enrollment in the school.

b. The need for belonging

All of us want to feel that we are accepted and that we are valuable persons whom others enjoy having around. When nonchurch families come into a church's weekday program, they want to feel that they are welcome. The board which takes steps to ensure that acceptance also plans for policy that helps these families feel that they are a part of the church's life. Some ways that this might be done are:

Family Adoption Plan

Names of new school families are matched with willing church families who "adopt" the new family. The church family may invite the new family to their home for dessert or they may arrange to visit the new family's home, telling them about the church programs. This personal invitation to join a church circle or to come to church with them on Sunday helps a new family feel wanted. Even if they are established in another church, they will appreciate learning about the church whose preschool they have chosen for their children. If they are new to the community, they may also appreciate general information about the town's or area's banks, stores, and shopping centers. The names of doctors, dentists, or baby-sitters may be just what they are looking for. Knowing they can call someone for information helps a new family feel more at ease in a new environment.

Welcome Committee

The board may look upon the church's outreach to new families in the school as so important that it develops policy for a committee to call upon the new family and welcome them. Being on this committee could be the specific duty of two or three of the board members, or it could be done by another church committee whose job is outreach or evangelism. It may sometimes be done by someone from the church staff if he or she has the time and is an outgoing, friendly person who enjoys working with new families.

A minister or DCE who regularly visits the classrooms when parents are bringing or picking up children helps new families feel welcome and helps them feel that the church cares about them.

COSTS OF STARTING A WEEKDAY PROGRAM

Getting started means taking a very close look at the furnishings that are already on hand in the classrooms that will be used for the weekday program. It is possible that these rooms will already have child-size tables and chairs in them. They may also have low shelves with a set of blocks, an easel, a doll and doll bed, and a stove and sink for a housekeeping center. What will you need to add? Look at the following lists of basics to guide you as you determine your needs.

List 1: Minimum equipment and supplies needed for a room that is already furnished
- record player
- records
- puzzles
- set of Legos
- set of Bristle Blocks
- magnifying glass
- magnets
- another doll
- 2 large riding trucks
- 4 small trucks and cars
- 1 set of plastic dishes
- dress-up clothes
- storybooks
- 3 reams 18" x 24" newsprint
- 1 ream 12" x 18" manila paper
- 24 packages 12" x 18" construction paper
- 2 packages markers
- 6 boxes large crayons
- 24 cans easel paint
- 6 long-handle paintbrushes
- 1 gallon glue
- 1 gallon paste
- collage materials
- 16 coat hooks
- 16 dishpans for cubbies
- 2 additional sets of shelves purchased from a teacher's supply store or homemade with only the lumber purchased

Younger children of two-and-a-half and three have different needs in terms of manipulatives than four- and five-year-old children. Very young children are apt to put small objects in their mouths, so large-size Legos and Bristle Blocks or Crystal Climbers would be excellent for these age groups. Wooden puzzles should be less complicated for children in the younger classes—between three and eight pieces.

Four- and five-year-olds have generally outgrown the need to put objects in their mouths. They also need manipulatives that help develop good eye-hand coordination. Some of the following would make good additions to a classroom for four- and five-year-olds:

beads and laces	Konnecto sets
play tiles	lacing boards
pegs and peg boards	puzzles—8 to 15 pieces
hammer and nail sets	(for threes and young fours)
wooden nuts and bolts	puzzles—18 to 27 pieces
	(for older fours and fives)

SETTING UP AN ADMINISTRATIVE BOARD

When setting up any interest center, it is wise to have enough equipment and supplies so that more than one child can work. It is good to plan for two to four children because they enjoy working together in small groups. They find it hard to wait for turns when there is a limited number of items in a center.

List 2: Minimum equipment for an unfurnished classroom
- basic items from list 1
- 2 tables
- 16 chairs
- easel
- stove
- sink
- doll bed
- 2 dolls
- cupboard
- table-and-chair set
- 2 open shelves
- blocks

Churches that have never had a weekday program will usually not have developed a playground for children. The following list represents the items needed for an outside play area.

List 3: Minimum equipment for an outdoor playground
- treated lumber for a sand box
- sand
- spoons, pots, pans, cans
- climbing tower made with treated lumber
- concrete trike path
- fence (4' high)
- 3 tricycles
- tires

If your church is developing a day care program, the cost of cots will need to be added to the list.

MEETING LICENSING STANDARDS

Because most states now require all programs for young children to be licensed, your church may need some alterations to bring the building into compliance with these licensing requirements. Some equipment or changes needed to meet most state and local licensing standards are:

2 doors in each classroom
fire and smoke alarm system
proof that existing carpeting and drapes are fire-resistant
doors with breaker bars that open outward

Some fire codes require that the building be constructed with two-hour fire walls and that hallways be of a certain width.

It is important that licensing requirements are examined in detail by the board very early in the planning stages of a new weekday program. Depending on the state in which

THE CHURCH-RELATED PRESCHOOL

you reside, they can vary from lax to stringent. Some of the more stringent ones designate the items of equipment that must appear in each classroom, for example, the number of musical or rhythm instruments or the number of push-pull toys. Meeting building and

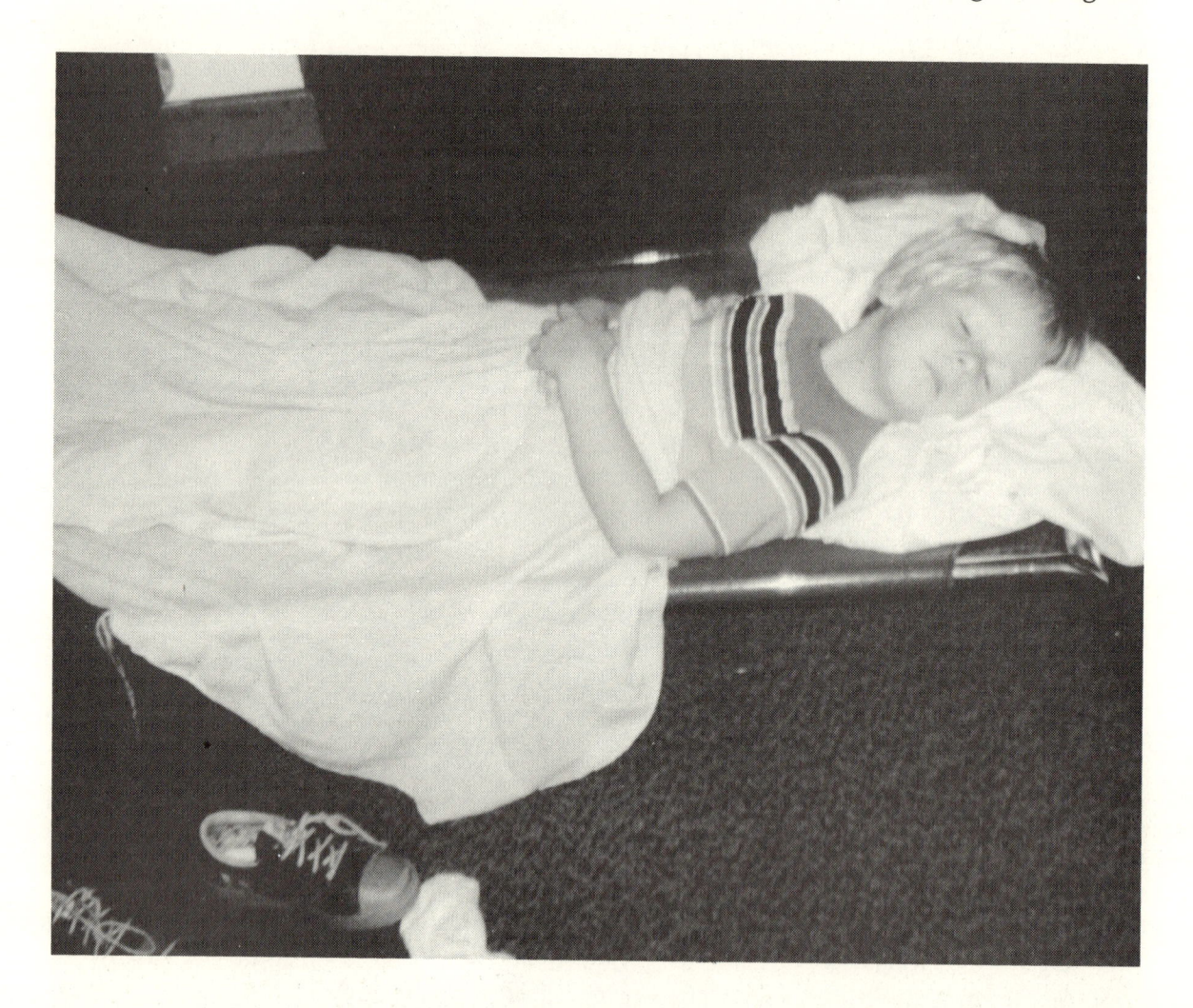

fire codes is usually a part of licensing requirements and this can represent an expenditure of a great deal of money for churches that are older. Kitchens frequently have to be remodeled to be brought up-to-date, sometimes with the addition of separate sinks for washing hands and for preparing food. Sewer lines occasionally need to be enlarged to meet health codes for day care programs. Some fire codes require that no more than one-half of a classroom be carpeted. Such a requirement can be a disappointment to a congregation that has just built a new church or remodeled an older one and carpeted every classroom.

THE WORK OF THE BOARD

The ongoing work of the board or committee is an outgrowth of the policy it establishes. For example, reviewing scholarship applications and granting them will be part of the

SETTING UP AN ADMINISTRATIVE BOARD

board's work if a scholarship policy has been established. Planning the parent education events and visiting new families in the program happen because a policy on ministry to families has been established. Preparing a monthly financial record and making sure that the weekday program is operating within the budget also fall within the realm of the board's responsibility. Hiring and making personnel changes each year comprise part of the work of the board.

In addition to responsibilities that arise from policy the board has established, two more areas exist. These are:

a. Reporting to the church
b. Evaluating the board

Part of the ongoing job of the board is to regularly inform the rest of the church about the activities and the needs of the weekday program. It includes making a verbal report to the members of the governing body of the church as well as having the minutes of meetings available to them. It involves writing articles for the church newspaper and, on occasion, sending news items to the town paper. This regular process of reporting enables the congregation to see the weekday program as a busy, happy, Christian environment where young children learn through play. Communication with the congregation brings to light

A board member who regularly takes part in the life of the weekday program can know firsthand what the program is like.

the needs of children and how the church meets those needs. The board does the public relations on behalf of the preschool and interprets the work of the program to the church.

After policies are decided upon, the board or committee should take steps to ensure that the policies are carried out. To do this, a means of evaluating itself should exist. For example, a monthly financial statement will present the board with a graphic picture of how well the school is staying within the budget. If the school is open nine months or twelve months a year, the financial statement can reflect the percentage spent and the percentage remaining in each budget category (one-ninth or one-twelfth for each month).

When a board looks at itself critically, it ensures that changes in policy have not crept into the ongoing nature of the weekday program and that the basic intent is still being carried out. See the following page for a sample of an evaluation form that could be used by the board.

A board needs a means of evaluating itself to know that, indeed, it is doing a good job. There will be areas where it can do better. An individual board can probably come up with more and different questions that reflect its own style and needs. Any board can grow when it takes a long, hard look at itself and realizes where more energy must be spent.

At times the written policy will prove to be inappropriate and should be changed with the board members' consent. For example, a teacher may require surgery and need far more time for recuperation than the allotted sick leave. Or, children enrolled in other programs in the church, such as the church's drop-in care, may need to be given a higher priority for enrolling in the preschool than the children of new families.

These changes in a board's bylaws or guidelines reflect the ongoing needs of the school. At no time should board members feel that the bylaws or policies are not changeable. They are simply a tool to get the job done.

COMMON MISCONCEPTIONS

Most congregations that have a weekday preschool program will have some common misconceptions about it. These ideas surface every now and then, and the director and board need to deal with misconceptions as soon as they know of them. There is no substitute for a well-informed congregation. Let us look at some of these misconceptions.

1. The Weekday Program Will Cost the Church a Lot of Money

Some persons worry that the increased use of electricity in lighting the classrooms will cause the church's bills to skyrocket. In reality, the biggest drain in electricity occurs on Sunday morning when the lights are turned on in the large sanctuary and, at the same time, in the fellowship hall, hallways, and all the other classrooms. Weekday use of lights in the preschool classrooms will be small in comparison to overall usage.

Most churches will turn on the heat or air conditioning during the week because the building will be used by the ministers, secretary, and other church staff. Janitors like to work with the heating or air conditioning on. Scout troops in the afternoons, women's meetings in the mornings, and all evening meetings will also use the utilities.

Studies that compare a church's utility bills during months when the weekday program is not in session (June, July, August, and half of December if it is a nine-month program)

Sample

SELF-EVALUATION FOR A BOARD

	Always	Most of the Time	Never
All teachers in the school meet educational standards decided upon by the board.	_____	_____	_____
All teachers are given sick leave according to policy.	_____	_____	_____
The school stays within its budget.	_____	_____	_____
The budget reflects the anticipated needs of the school.	_____	_____	_____
Actual class size is the optimum agreed upon.	_____	_____	_____
Families who are getting scholarship help receive enough to meet their needs.	_____	_____	_____
It is known that scholarship help is available if needed.	_____	_____	_____
The priority of acceptance into the school enables new families to find a place.	_____	_____	_____
The classes offered represent the biggest need in each age group.	_____	_____	_____
The health policy is adequate to keep illness at a minimum.	_____	_____	_____
The church's curriculum materials are available to teachers.	_____	_____	_____
Teachers are using curriculum which is compatible with the church's Sunday curriculum.	_____	_____	_____
Members have long enough terms on the board to be effective.	_____	_____	_____
Board members' abilities are used effectively.	_____	_____	_____
Board members act as liaison between the church and the school.	_____	_____	_____
Board members do public relations for the school.	_____	_____	_____
Board members stand behind and support the staff at the school.	_____	_____	_____
Board members refrain from taking information about the families beyond the meeting.	_____	_____	_____
School families are aware of other church programs.	_____	_____	_____
School families feel welcome in the church.	_____	_____	_____
Educational events are planned for parents of children in the weekday program.	_____	_____	_____
Educational events are held often enough to meet the needs of families.	_____	_____	_____

with months when it is in operation indicate very little change in consumption of electricity and in heating or cooling costs.

To counteract this misconception, it is helpful to invite members of the congregation to look at actual utility bills, comparing months when the school is closed. The period of time before the school opened can be compared with bills for the months after the school began operating. A representative from the electric company could be contacted for an opinion about costs.

2. *The Weekday Program Makes a Lot of Money*

It is true that weekday programs usually charge tuition. This very fact of charging is seen by some people in the congregation as meaning that the weekday program takes in money, and such people give little thought to how much must be spent on operating costs. A good program neither makes money nor costs a church money. It simply breaks even and takes in enough to pay teachers' salaries, buy equipment and supplies, provide for speakers for parent meetings, and have available some money for professional training for the staff.

To counteract this misconception the congregation needs to be informed about the expenses of the weekday program. This information can be presented regularly at the meeting of the church's governing body. A church newsletter item about the costs of the weekday program may also be appropriate.

3. *Preschool Is Just Play*

The implication here is that learning does not occur during play. The misconception arises out of the notion some people have that a teaching situation means "lessons," usually with children sitting quietly at desks and listening to a teacher.

Every effort should be made to help a congregation understand how small children utilize play to learn. Certainly not everyone has been trained to be a teacher; even those who have taught older children may find it hard to understand the learning process in a young child. Few older adults attended preschool themselves as children and most have only memories of being required to sit out a school year in one seat, listening to one teacher in front of the group. The term *interest center* may be as foreign to some persons as the concept of learning through play.

A slide program for the congregation can graphically illustrate how children learn through play.

4. *The Weekday Program Does Not Teach Religion*

A member of the congregation, observing the church weekday program in action, would find a large block of time set aside for inside play (free-choice time). Some children would be building with blocks, others would be enjoying an art activity, and others would be engaged in pretending they were a family feeding a doll and washing dishes. Some children may be crowded around a science table where a collection of worms are spinning cocoons.

As the observation continued, the member of the congregation would see a long block of time set aside for outside play. Shorter time periods would be reserved for snack and cleanup and for a group time together. This group time may include a discussion about the worms on the science table or questions about the story that the teacher has read.

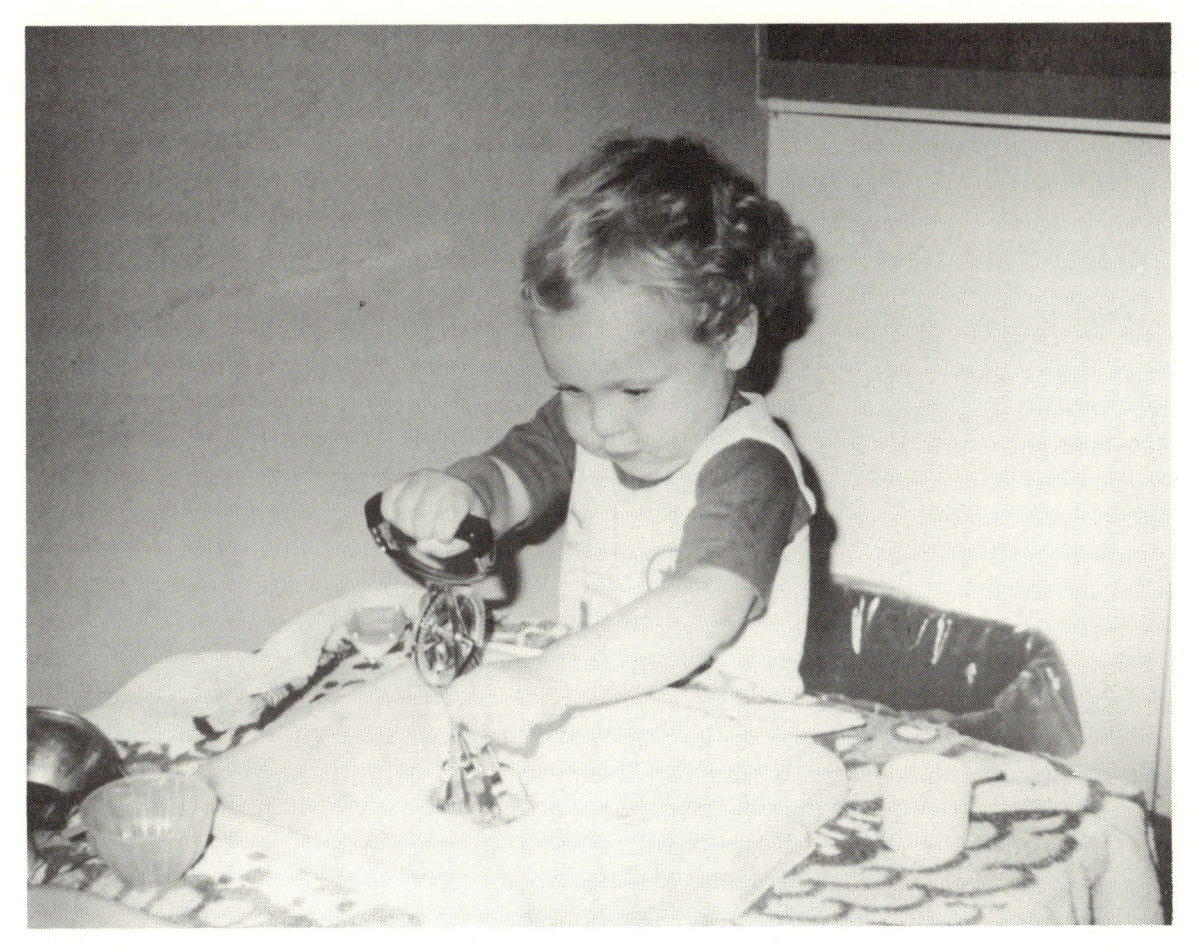

Because not a lot of time is allocated for Bible stories or learning Bible verses, our observer may conclude that religion is not being taught. However, young children do not have very long attention spans and are not yet interested in stories about events that do not have meaning for them. They delight in the here-and-now stories of their own experience: home and family life, animals and bugs, cars, trucks, and building construction.

It is through the everyday activities of snack time, indoor and outdoor play that religion is being taught as teachers and students are involved in Christian living together. Children are met on their level, and teachers show, by example, Christ's way of love, acceptance, and forgiveness. Religion is not studied; it is lived. Later, when the children are older, they will be able to handle a more formal study situation.

Some people feel that having "chapel" once a week is tangible evidence that religion is being taught in the preschool. However, most children's chapel services still deal in the abstract, and the effort will often be beyond their comprehension. Young children cannot draw analogies or appreciate moralistic mini-sermons. Teachers have to teach in a way that reaches children, rather than offer programs that please adults.

The church newsletter can again be the most effective way of reaching others. Articles about children learning best by doing, rather than by being told, are helpful and educational. Words are quickly forgotten, but when a child actually experiences love and forgiveness, the concepts come alive.

Here is an example of a church newsletter that was prepared to help adults understand how young children think, particularly about Christmas and all of its meaning.

*As You and Your Young Children
Prepare for Christmas*

We parents want so much to impart to our children the real meaning of Christmas, to help them understand God's precious gift to us, and to have them grow in understanding of the good news of God's love. How can we best do that? Let's look at how young children are unique in their approach to learning.

Their concept of time is not learned until age five or so. It is hard for them to wait for Christmas. Preparations begun early in the month, such as mailing gifts and baking, only intensify the wait. Children are apt to be excitable and stimulated. They could wait more easily if less emphasis was put on these events and if the tree went up only a week ahead of time.

For very young children, the holiday is more easily understood after it is over. The Christmas story will have more meaning if we tell it again several times after Christmas.

Children learn best through play. Having an unbreakable crèche to play with will enable them to act out the Christmas story through their dramatization of it.

Children learn through experience. It is important for them to see, touch, taste, and do. Having them participate in the giving of gifts to family, friends, and the needy is a better way of learning about sharing than reading a story about it.

Children think and speak in concrete, literal terms. At this stage in their lives they have a hard time distinguishing reality from unreality, or what is real from what is fantasy. Do we really want to teach that reindeer can fly? Some stories may better wait until after the fifth birthday.

Young children have very short attention spans. The Christmas story may have more meaning at this point in their lives if we tell it, rather than read it, holding them close to us as we do.

The message and meaning of the Christmas story are best taught through attitudes and relationships in addition to telling the story. At a later time they will learn more about places and events. Symbolism, chronology, and history become important when children can think abstractly, beginning at around age eight.

As small children are caught up in the love we have for them and for each other, they learn about God's gift of love.

5. Anyone Can Teach Young Children

This misconception encourages the low pay that is common to teachers in the profession. Very few persons realize that early childhood education and child development are separate disciplines, just as chemistry and physics are. Teachers of young children have been thought of as baby-sitters. The training, experience, and commitment of people in this field are tremendous, and we all need to dispel the myth of nonprofessionalism.

Educating not only the church congregation but the public in general is a priority. Items in the local paper and the church newsletter help. Some teachers regularly use a bulletin board outside the classroom door which lists the title of that week's unit; the activities that will be used to develop the unit, such as the stories, songs, games, and finger plays chosen; the objects that will be displayed on the science table; and the manipulatives and art activities that will accompany the unit. The director can add condensed versions of these activities in the church newsletter so the congregation's members can grasp the planning and effort involved in teaching very young children.

Teachers' and the director's diplomas and other letters of achievement displayed in the preschool office will also make a statement. The school's parent handbook can comment on the training and experience of the school staff.

Such misconceptions about a church's weekday program are common to every congregation. Sometimes the misconceptions are voiced as complaints. The natural reaction is a defensive one. However, it is always better to anticipate that misconceptions may occur and to make a concerted effort to keep the congregation well informed. Regular items in the church newsletter are a must and should be considered part of the director's and board's responsibilities. Slide shows can be presented at the church family night suppers. Posters in the church narthex can portray life in the preschool classrooms. Look for opportunities to share news of the weekday program with different church groups. For example, use decorations made by the children for the men's breakfast, or have the senior citizens group visit the preschool at snack time when the children will have prepared the treats.

We live in a mobile society and should anticipate that people will come and go within a congregation. Perhaps a good job of keeping everyone well informed was done all year. But each year is a new year, and each year the job must begin again.

THE DIRECTOR

The key staff person that the board decides upon is the director. Although this person is usually hired for this one position, the director may also combine the job with other church duties such as being the minister of children's work or the director of Christian education. If the weekday program is very small, the director may also teach a preschool class.

The kind of person who will be most effective in this job has good skills in working with people, is a caring person, takes time to listen, and knows how to help adults grow to their full potential. This type of person has the capacity to be an effective administrator.

Of course, the board will want to find a director who has a degree in child development or early childhood education or its equivalent. College grades, however, may not be a good indicator of success in the job. Another consideration is the applicant's skill as a classroom teacher. The key ingredient to being an effective director is the ability to get along well with people and to motivate others to be the best they can be.

The director should be a person with a vision. But such a person should not be the type who sees people as obstacles on the way to the perfect school. Rather, the director will accept people where they are, knowing that all persons, adults as well as children, can change and grow and come to see the vision also. A good director will help others catch the vision, so that it becomes theirs as well.

An effective director understands the learning process in adults as well as in children and creates a learning situation for the teachers as well as for the board.

A director is a manager with a philosophy of education, and the school will reflect that philosophy. Each director has a unique way of dealing with people and becomes a role model for teachers as well as parents.

THE DIRECTOR'S RELATIONSHIP TO THE BOARD

Some directors serve as ex officio members of the board. Some have voting rights. However, the director's main relationship is advisory in nature. The director's work with the board is approached from two areas.

THE DIRECTOR

1. Keeping the Board Informed About the School

The director makes certain each board member has a copy of all notes that the children take home to their parents. Copies are brought to the monthly board meetings. Notes could be mailed to each member on the same day the children take theirs home. Parent members of the board will naturally receive their notes from their children. Board members who also have other church duties (such as the minister or director of Christian education) can be handed theirs. This would leave only a few that would have to be mailed. The director refers briefly to these notes when making a report, knowing that human nature being what it is, not everyone will have read them all.

The director's report to the board should be included on the agenda of every board meeting. This report also has the purpose of informing the members about school happenings. Included will be big events such as hearing and vision screening and parent meetings that have been scheduled. Small events such as moving a child from one class to another, the need for a piece of playground equipment, or a sand delivery are reported. The board is informed of all matters pertaining to the school, but the director does not ask for permission to take care of these. Once money is appropriated for supplies and equipment in the yearly budget, the director works within the budget and buys what is needed. It is the director's job to take care of the day-to-day operation of the school.

2. Educating the Board About Young Children

The director looks for ways to tell the board about the needs of young children and how best to meet them. In planning for classes, for example, the director suggests a pupil-teacher ratio that works well for each age group. In reporting on how holidays are celebrated, the director includes some information about children's apprehensions and fears. During curriculum discussions, comments made by the director remind board members that children think concretely rather than abstractly. These bits of information allow the board to make better-informed decisions about policy.

Because board members change every year or two, the director should remind them on occasion about the need for confidentiality. Some information that is discussed should never be repeated. Examples include requests for scholarship help or a child dropping out of school because of a family problem, such as a divorce. Even casual remarks about children and their families should never be passed on to others outside the board. Gossip can cause information to be twisted and bring embarrassment to many persons.

The director also must be alert to the different areas of responsibility of board members. New members coming on the board should be presented with bylaws and guidelines which help them understand their job. Their apprenticeship can be enhanced if the director will spend some time with new board members at the beginning of their term, explaining the work the director does. An invitation to visit the school and see it in action will enable the board members to appreciate the scope of a director's job. Such a visit will also help them become familiar with the whole school operation.

In spite of best intentions of everyone, misunderstandings can occur and occasionally there will be conflicts. Such differences between board members or between board and director can be avoided if it is clear that each has separate and distinct areas of responsibility. For example, board members do not have to feel that it is their duty to order equipment or supplies or decide on the activities in which the children participate. Nor should they feel that they are capable of making value judgments about aspects of the school curriculum without appropriate study and help. The following example illustrates how this can happen. It took place in a large church with a weekday preschool.

A parent happened to meet a board member after church and complained about water play in the preschool. The parent did not like for her child to play in water. The little boy, however, enjoyed the activity and played happily at the water table. The board member agreed with the parent that water should not be available to the children (value judgment about curriculum) and brought the matter before the board. As a result, the teacher resigned, feeling that the board was not supportive of her and did not comprehend the value of water play.

In this example, it would have been far better for the board member to have said to the parent, "I know how you feel about that, but I am sure there must be some value in water play or the teacher would not include it in the program. Why don't you talk to the teacher about it?" Such an answer would have supported the feelings of the parent while affirming the teacher, and it would have offered a suggestion for resolving the conflict.

Directors have clearly defined areas of responsibility. So do boards.

THE DIRECTOR'S NEEDS

The director of a church preschool is placed in the unique position of having no one else on the church staff or the school staff with the same kinds of problems and needs. There is simply no similar position within the same building. Teachers have other teachers with whom they can relate; a board member has other board members. Even ministers and directors of Christian education view their situation as more allied with one another than with the preschool director.

Directors sometimes find themselves with a very alone-on-an-island feeling in the midst of a hectic day. The best support will come from directors of other preschools. They have experienced and solved problems about registration, budgeting, church relationships, teacher training, and parent education. They will offer ideas and suggestions, some of which will be very helpful. Most of all, they will be persons with whom the director can relate. Some directors form groups to meet for a social hour and salad lunch and talk. Other groups may be more formal, meeting regularly with a speaker each time. This support network of directors meets a very real need. One director formed such a group by asking all the directors from churches in the area to come to her church. Each brought a brown-bag lunch. The agenda included sharing information about tuition fees and staff salaries. The directors found they had much in common and have continued to meet once a month. Their agendas have included enrollment procedure, open house ideas, and sharing parent handbooks. Their lunch fare has grown to more elegant potluck dishes, and once they even splurged on a caterer. They see little of one another at other times but know each is as close as a phone call if they need help.

The director's needs center around the following areas:

1. Directors Need to Know That Their Boards Support Them

They need a pat on the back occasionally. They need to be aware that their board not only wholeheartedly approves of how they go about their job, but will come to their defense if anyone questions why they do what they do. One director once asked to have small, child-size toilets installed in the classrooms. Some members of the church property committee questioned why spending the money for the toilets was necessary. The chairman of the preschool board informed them about how much easier it would be for the children to use the bathroom. The property committee had simply never considered that to be a problem. Support came because the chairman helped others see the director's point of view.

2. Directors Need Time and Money for Their Own Continuing Education

Some boards add a budget line item for the teachers' professional training. However, an alert board, tuned in to its director's needs, also adds money for the director's educational development. The needs of the director may not be the same as the needs of the teachers. Most workshops for teachers deal with new ideas for art and music activities, handling behavior problems in the classroom, or gross motor training. Although directors enjoy and benefit from keeping up-to-date with new ideas for the classroom, they may also wish to add refresher courses from a university or summer school for more in-depth study. Courses in management and supervision can be helpful. If such classes are taken during the school year, arrangements should be made by the board for some office help to lighten the director's work load. A director will be an even better director if time is made for participation in extra training.

3. Directors Need a Monthly Financial Statement

This financial statement gives the director an immediate picture of how well the budget is being adhered to. It shows if the school is on target with money spent for substitutes or equipment or juice and crackers. It shows whether funds are available for one more speaker for a parent meeting. Because it is the director's job to operate within the budget, this financial statement represents a guideline for decisions on school operation.

4. Directors Need a Car Allowance

It is the director who must make quick trips around town for extra juice or a book about an upcoming holiday or glue or film for photographs. The director might also want to observe other preschools and first grades. This is all school business, frequently done on personal time after the school has closed. It is only fair that the director be compensated for the trips.

5. Directors Need a Petty Cash Fund

Directors frequently make trips for supplies. If a petty cash fund is not provided, supplies must be paid for out of the director's pocket. If an item is delivered to the school COD, the director may write a check off his or her personal checking account. Over a month's time this can amount to a large outlay of cash and can mean that the director's money has become a working account of the school. Most director's salaries are stretched to the limit with these expenditures. A large enough petty cash fund can be a welcome relief.

6. Directors Need a System for Handling Burnout

Being director of a school is a high-stress job. A director deals with one problem after another and must give undivided attention to each one.

A typical day may include meeting with several visitors who want to observe the classes and apply to the school for admission of a child, listening to the visitors describe their children in detail, giving advice about placement, observing a child in one of the classes, conferring with teachers about the child, counseling a mother about temper tantrums, giving an opinion to a teacher about the relationship between diet and hyperactivity, removing a splinter from under the fingernail of a crying child, making phone calls to arrange for a field trip, and returning a call regarding a speaking engagement.

Although these activities are not stressful in themselves, the ongoing frequency of them, hour after hour in a director's day, takes its toll. If the director works a full day rather than a half day, there still are school errands to run after the doors are finally closed in the late afternoon. Evenings bring phone calls from teachers seeking advice on handling problems. The next day may begin at 7:00 A.M. with lining up substitutes for the day.

Some directors do not last long on the job. Most move on to other careers after a few years. Those who do endure discover ways of handling the long hours and numerous problems. It may be that one afternoon a week away from the school will be necessary. Or, perhaps a two- or three-day trip to an early childhood convention in another city will bring enough change of pace. One director who has stayed with her preschool for sixteen years admits to taking a day off "whenever school gets to be too much for me." She even enjoys the luxury of going in late on occasion.

Another director and her husband are the lucky owners of a weekend place. From school's closing on Friday until Monday morning, they enjoy the quiet country sounds.

THE DIRECTOR

"Sometimes I just sit and stare at the woods," she confides. If a person enjoys the profession and wants to stay in it, change-of-pace activities must be searched out, even if the change of pace is doing nothing. The director should not feel guilty about taking time off from work if it is needed, because it is necessary.

A good board will support the director in the need to establish a routine that gives some relief from the problems and long hours. Some directors do not even have a lunch hour but often grab a sandwich in the midst of a meeting or other job. Some burnout can be cured by a sabbatical or a year away from school, a method used by college professors. Many directors have no vacations. Even a month's leave of absence can renew and restore a tired director. Another drastic but effective method is to exchange schools with another director for a period of time, just as some ministers exchange pulpits.

7. Directors Need Freedom

A teacher who was recently made director at her church preschool was asked, "How are you liking your new job?" She confided with honesty, "I love being boss!"

This need to do things in one's own way and to shape the school according to an ideal picture one has in mind is present with most directors. There are some teachers who would not accept the advancement to director at all. These are good teachers who are content in the classroom. "I wouldn't want that job!" they exclaim vehemently, knowing how much of a strain it could be.

A good director not only accepts responsibility well but seeks it out, knowing that is what is needed to bring to fruition one's dreams for the school. A director needs and accepts independence and is comfortable with Harry Truman's motto, "The buck stops here."

A board should give the director this autonomy. Once the board has developed policies for the school, its members should be comfortable with letting the director carry them out. Difficulties arise when a board tries to do the director's job (which is supervising) or the director tries to do the board's job (which is policy making). Boards are made up of well-meaning people, valuable contributors to the school from many areas of business, finance, personnel, and education. Because they are also parents, it may be hard for them not to offer advice, which is helpful sometimes and unneeded at others. For example, it may be difficult for some of them to understand that the learning styles and developmental needs of very young children can be quite different from those of the elementary or high-school student.

It can also be very tempting for a new director to come into an existing preschool situation and try to change school policy too quickly. Because policy has been thoughtfully considered by many people over a long period of time, the new director should proceed with caution. Time and patience are qualities that can work well for the director as the board is led through a learning process of considering new ideas.

LEADERSHIP STYLES

When considering what kind of person makes the most effective director, let us look at the following examples:

School #1
The director resigned, and one of the teachers was appointed to the position. She usually had worn comfortable slacks, clean blouses, and low-heeled shoes when she worked with children in the classroom. However, after being appointed director, she felt it necessary to "dress up" because she thought it brought dignity to the office. She chose "Sunday" clothes: dresses that were dry cleanable instead of washable.

Because there was so much work to do, she found that keeping her office door closed gave her more time to think. Teachers who once enjoyed talking with her no longer stopped in to visit.

She also knew that teachers work very hard, so she determined to solve most of the school's problems by herself. She did not want to bother them with deciding who should use the playground first. She made out a schedule showing when each teacher could have a playground time. She also felt she could save the teachers some time by writing curricula for them.

Soon the teachers felt the curriculum did not really meet the needs of the children they had in class. They grumbled about the playground time they had been assigned because it did not seem to suit their daily schedule. By the end of the year, four out of a staff of five teachers decided to look for a new school in which to teach.

School #2
A new director who had recently finished college was appointed. In fact, he had several degrees. He felt he really knew all about early childhood education. He arrived a few weeks before school opened and reorganized everything. He worked out the curriculum for each age group and assigned teachers to certain duties in the school such as storage room cleaning. He developed programs for staff meetings for the whole year. When he wished to communicate with the staff, he sent memos to them. At the end of the semester, four out of a staff of five teachers decided to look for a new school in which to teach.

School #3
The director had been at the school as long as most of the teachers. Visitors who came to the school had difficulty finding her because she was frequently in the classrooms. She sometimes wore an apron just as some of the teachers did. When water spilled on the floor under the water table, she would mop it up if the classroom teachers were busy. She had the teachers decide on their own playground times, and together they worked on the curriculum for the year. As usual, everyone signed contracts at the end of the year.

The above examples are simplified to illustrate how different styles of leadership can affect teachers. The director in school #1 tried her best but failed to understand the needs of her group. The director of school #2 had ego needs that prevented him from being effective. Dr. Thomas Gordon, in his book *Leader Effectiveness Training* (New York: Bantam Books, 1980), states, "Effective leaders must behave in such a way that they come to be perceived almost as another group member; at the same time they must help all group members feel as free as the leader to make contributions and perform needed functions in the group." Thus a director who is able to be as democratic as possible by giving the staff a voice in much of the decision making can turn the group into happier, more creative, and more productive individuals. We all want to feel we have a voice in our destiny by choosing curricula and activities which best suit the children with whom we work or by choosing programs which we believe will strengthen our professional development. We tend to resent a leader who presumes to know what is best for us, or one who does not give us an opportunity to grow by doing. A group of teachers, if allowed, are more apt to subscribe to the school's philosophy if they feel they have had a voice in its shaping. If a director's dress and manner send the message that all teachers are subordinates, then they in turn feel less acceptable.

A good director will try to include teachers in as much of the decision making as possible. For example, decisions that can be shared include:
   curriculum planning
   end-of-the-year duties
   care of the storage closet
   playground times
   playground rules
   equipment needed for playground and in the classroom
   scheduling
   in-service training
   parent programs
   children who arrive too early or too late
   books needed
   responsibility of aides
You will be able to add much more to the list.

Not every decision can be a group decision, however, and the director has to refrain from enlisting teachers in decisions that have to do with matters of policy which have been developed by the board. Some of these include decisions about:
   salaries
   tuition rates
   admission and attendance
   personnel
   budget
   health requirements
Directors have to make decisions regarding space, equipment, and programs upon which licensing depends. Other decisions involve defining the policies which the board has established. A democratic approach with teachers encourages positive relationships, fosters the growth of each one on the staff, and leads to greater understanding of the school's goals.

WRITING A JOB DESCRIPTION FOR THE DIRECTOR

The director's job is unique in the overall context of the church. There is no one else with duties and responsibilities that are quite like the director's. The preschool board's concept of the director's role will be reflected in the job description that it decides upon. Such a job description will cover general areas of responsibility because the board may not know specifics about all the work a director does. A board can draw up areas of accountability that are expected to be covered by the director, and the director can best determine the particular tasks which fulfill that accountability.

Writing a job description for the director is directly related to how the board perceives the weekday program's goals and plans. In turn, persons applying for the job of director have some perceptions of what the job should entail.

First of all, it can be assumed that anyone applying for a director's job knows how to be a director. Therefore specific tasks or duties are not outlined in the job description. Areas are outlined for which the director will be held accountable. It is expected that the director will see to it that the areas are covered—either by doing the jobs directly or by delegating jobs to an assistant or to the teachers.

Next, a board needs to look at how it will know if the areas of accountability have actually been fulfilled. For example, if the director is expected to operate the school within the budget (area of accountability), then the board will know this area has been fulfilled when the school year ends and there has not been any overspending. It is not up to the board members to tell the director how to do it. Their concern should be only that it is done. It should not concern them how many hours are spent on finding bargains in order to keep some costs low or that the director does not spend many hours on the problem at all. A board should simply want to see results.

Here is another example. Suppose a board wants the staff to have in-service training as an area of accountability. How this is accomplished is not the board's concern; it is up to the director. The director may enroll the staff in several workshops each year, or the weekly staff meeting may be a time of study and learning. A board knows this area has been fulfilled when evidence of enrollment in the workshops or the books or topics covered during the weekly staff meeting are shared with the board.

With the plans and goals of the weekday program in mind, most boards will want to cover the following areas when writing a job description for the director:
1. A general statement about the scope of the job
2. The organizational relationships, or to whom the director will be accountable
3. Specific areas of accountability

Use the following sample job description to begin thinking of those things that should be included in the director's job description for your program.

Sample

JOB DESCRIPTION FOR THE DIRECTOR

1. The director will be responsible for the administration and coordination of the weekday program.
2. The director will be directly responsible to the preschool board.
3. The director will
   a. supervise staff, schedule, and curriculum
   b. implement a program for parents
   c. serve as a member of the preschool board
   d. interview prospective teachers and make recommendations to the board
   e. evaluate teacher performance
   f. keep medical and developmental records
   g. order equipment and supplies
   h. supervise registration process and place children in classes according to their needs and abilities.
   i. supervise meeting and maintaining licensing requirements

THE DIRECTOR

The educational requirements and experience that a board desires are not part of a job description. A job description is simply what it says it is: a description of a job. The salary or other terms of employment are not part of a job description but are a separate document, a contract of employment.

PROGRAM EVALUATION

In addition to conducting regular evaluations of the board, director, and teachers, it is helpful to do an objective and critical evaluation of the total program. The director, in cooperation with the board, is primarily responsible for conducting this evaluation. Such an evaluation should reflect the school's philosophy and expectations. It gives everyone—staff, board, and director—a means of looking at the program to see if the goals for the school are being met. An evaluation of the program shows where changes need to be made as well as offering an opportunity to appreciate the weekday program by graphically illustrating how well it is doing.

Following is a sample evaluation form which reflects the goals one school established for itself. As you look at the goals for your weekday program, you may find some things you want to add to this form and some items you will want to change. Your program evaluation form should reflect the goals you have established for your weekday program.

Sample
PROGRAM EVALUATION

	Yes	No	Sometimes

Physical Setup

1. Is each classroom large enough for the number of children?
2. Is there a bathroom available to the children?
3. Can the teacher supervise the bathroom and the class at the same time?
4. Are the rooms well lighted?
5. Do rooms smell fresh when you come in?
6. Are there danger spots in the room such as:
   sharp hooks or nails?
   thumbtacks in pictures?
   blocked stairways?
7. Is the playground enclosed?
8. Are the slides the right height for the age of the child?
9. Is there ample equipment in the playground?

Children's Health

1. Do the children look well?
2. Are children sent home if they become ill at school?
3. Is there an isolation room for a child who becomes ill at school?
4. Do the children have an outside time?
5. Is there a balance in the schedule between quiet time and active time?
6. Is there at least one teacher and one assistant with every group?
7. Are there no more than eighteen children in any group?
8. Do the younger children have a small group?

	Yes	No	Sometimes

9. Are bathroom visits handled in a matter-of-fact way?
10. Is the bathroom door open?

Relationships with Parents

1. Do parents come to the room to pick up children?
2. Does the teacher take time to say a few words to parents?
3. Is the director available to talk to parents?
4. Are there programs for parent education?
5. Are parent-teacher conferences regularly scheduled?

Teachers

1. Do teachers appear well adjusted and stable?
2. Is there a good feeling among staff members?
3. Have teachers planned interesting activities and environments for children?

Relationships with Children

1. Are children allowed to express their true feelings?
2. Are directions phrased positively?
3. Are there loving relationships?
4. Do teachers encourage the development of property rights?
5. Can a child have a toy as long as needed?
6. Is a shy child given helpful suggestions for entering a group?
7. Is positive redirection used for discipline?
8. Do the children appear busy and happy?

Creativity

1. Are children free to make what they want rather then copying patterns most of the time?
2. Is there opportunity to talk at snack time and at circle time?
3. Do teachers encourage creativity rather than interfere with it?

TEACHERS

Ideal teachers are those who are happy, warm, accepting, well-informed about how children learn and develop, and knowledgeable about how to establish a good emotional climate in the classroom. Ideal teachers feel comfortable with the school philosophy and look upon it as a reflection of their own. They have a high regard for other staff members and see each person as contributing to the ongoing development of all the children.

Everyone would like to hire the ideal teacher. Such a person is more important to the program than enough space or fancy equipment. How is a teacher found who brings to the classroom these desirable qualities? The church may not be located in an area of town where there are many people who have majored in child development or early childhood education in college. Certain personality traits are more important than college degrees in choosing a teacher of young children. Following is a profile of a good teacher.

1. *The Teacher Is Flexible*

A teacher who demands too much structure in the daily classroom routine probably will not be as effective as we would like. Although orderliness is desirable, too much of it can be inhibiting for young children. For example, the teacher who demands that paintbrushes always be wiped against the side of paint jars before a child paints may squelch the creative process, although showing the child how to cut down on paint drips may be welcome information. It is the degree to which a teacher demands adherence to the need for less mess that determines effectiveness. Inflexibility may exhibit itself in someone else as the inability to relinquish ideas for a theme when it is obvious the children are not interested. Good teaching begins with the children's interests. One such teacher, who had worked for hours the night before on costumes of biblical characters, found herself very disappointed when the class showed no interest in acting out a Bible story. Interest was still centered on a toy dinosaur that a child had brought to school. A more effective approach to learning would have been for the teacher to put away the costumes until such a time when interest was there. Since interest was keen on dinosaurs, projects related to them would have been the starting point for learning about them to take place. Interest in the biblical story could be stimulated by a trip to the DCE's office to see pictures of children in biblical lands, or it could occur when nativity figures are introduced at Christmastime. A flexible teacher picks up on the children's interest and knows how to introduce worthwhile themes by arousing that interest.

2. The Teacher Is Willing to Grow

We feel comfortable hiring a teacher with a backlog of ideas with which he or she can begin. Such a person may have developed some themes with accompanying songs, finger plays, and stories. There will be art projects and ideas for the science table or homemaking center that enhance the theme. However, some teachers get stuck and use the same ideas and resources year after year. These individuals usually are unwilling to look at a fresh approach and shun going to workshops and conferences. They project an I-know-everything-already point of view.

The teacher who can become excited with new ideas is refreshing for the children and the staff to be around. This person is constantly adding to a "bag of tricks" and discarding techniques that have grown stale.

Such teachers are willing to look at new theories of learning and try them out. They may decide old ways are better, but the very process of being open to new approaches has stretched their minds. They may try out new ways of handling difficult children. They are always on the lookout for new books and are excited about new ideas.

3. The Teacher Is Warm and Affectionate with Children

A person who walks into this teacher's room sees frequent hugs being given. There is always a lap available into which a child can snuggle. If the teacher is sitting on the floor, four or more children enjoy the lap and the closeness with their teacher and with one another. There is a lot of eye contact between teacher and children. A smile and perhaps a wink reminds those across the room that their teacher is aware of them and cares about them.

Such teachers know how much overt affection a child needs. They may simply stand by a shy child, not saying much, perhaps with a hand resting lightly on the child's shoulder. The touch reminds the child, "I am here. We don't have to talk if you're not ready for it, but I'll be with you until you are ready to move out on your own." Another child may need a big bear hug many times during the day. The teacher's arms are always open when the child is ready to express and receive affection.

Children know the teacher cares about them by the comments the teacher makes. "That's a neat building, Tommy." "You've made a blue picture, Jamie. I like the way the color goes all over the paper!" Caring is expressed by remembering what a child has worked on earlier in the day. "You climbed right up the slide today and came down!" "You made such a tall building when you worked with blocks this morning!" These comments not only show the children that they are cared about but also increase their self-esteem.

Because children thrive best in an atmosphere of love, the "cold fish" kind of teacher is best avoided. Children are more aloof when the teacher does not respond to their overtures. When children do not feel cared for, they in turn do not develop a caring feeling about one another. This kind of class exhibits more bickering and more overt fighting.

TEACHERS

4. The Teacher Gets Along with Other Staff Members and Grows with Teamwork and Shared Leadership

It is important for teachers to work in a climate of mutual respect. Growth happens when there is a sharing of ideas, for from such an atmosphere come even better ideas. Teachers who work with other teachers who care about one another also offer and receive support when they need it. When they give of themselves to one another, they receive a lot in return. These teachers are the kind who stay year after year. They have no need to job hop because they would rather be where they are.

Young children do best in a classroom where there are two or more teachers. It is important that these teachers have the ability to work well together. The whole class benefits from good teamwork and shared leadership.

5. The Teacher Is Accepting of Parents

Some teachers may come with excellent academic records and with a repertoire of ideas that will be of interest to children. However, if they are shy and reticent with parents, they will not be as effective.

Working with parents is every bit as important as working with children. Some parents are shy and reticent themselves, and a teacher who is at ease with other adults will know how to make the initial approach with these parents so they will feel comfortable and welcome. In fact, the teacher who is accepting by nature helps parents feel that they have found someone in whom they can confide.

6. The Teacher Has a Sense of Humor

Good teachers are able to laugh at themselves as well as laugh with others. The ability to see the bright side helps a teacher be more relaxed and easygoing. A teacher with a good sense of humor also helps children see more than one view of a situation. The general feeling in the classroom is more relaxed and joyful.

7. The Teacher Is Alert to a Child's Optimum Learning Time

Some educators call this the "teachable moment." Children do not always learn what and when we would like for them to learn. We can plan for hours and assemble all sorts of activities, but a child's interest and curiosity may be elsewhere. A young child learns best when a teacher zeroes in on curiosity and interest as they happen. For example, as a three-year-old pours water from one container to another such a teacher talks about the concepts of *full, empty, too much,* and *not enough.*

8. The Teacher Knows That the Teaching of Concepts Is More Important Than Rote Learning

As teachers work with young children, they are not only focusing on the "teachable moment," they are also helping the children think by helping them grasp concepts. The concept of what five forks and five knives are is more important than counting to five.

Being able to recognize that the words *horse* and *horn* begin with the "h" sound is more important than memorizing the alphabet.

Intellectual growth is swift during the preschool years because it is during this time that children develop concepts. Concepts of color, number, time, space, size, and class are formed as children play. For example, if a two-year-old finds a box of buttons of assorted sizes and colors the child may feel them, let them fall through the fingers, drop them, and even want to taste them (which is a problem because of the danger of swallowing them). This play is not random; it is for the purpose of learning about buttons. The concepts that a child will develop will be that buttons are round, feel smooth, and have no taste. When the same child is an older three- or four-year-old, the concepts of roundness, smoothness, and taste will not be as interesting because they are already understood and accepted. A four-year-old will be interested in sorting and classifying. The buttons will be dumped out of the box and the child will sort each according to color, with the red ones in one pile, the yellow ones in another, and so on. Or, the buttons may be sorted according to size—all small ones together and all large ones together. Learning these concepts of color and size is enhanced when teachers help children with labels or names of properties and objects.

"You have all the *red* buttons together. Do the pink ones go in a separate pile?"

"These are all *tiny* buttons."

"These are really *huge* buttons!"

We, as teachers, also strengthen concept formation when we provide varied classroom experiences. For example, one class had Pet Day, when two children and their parents could bring pets from home for a short visit. One pet was a tiny kitten, the other a large dog.

"How are these pets alike?" asked the teacher. The answers included:

"They both have fur."

"They both have ears."

"They both have legs."

"How many legs?" the teacher asked. The children counted.

"They have four," echoed the teacher. "They are both *animals.*"

When a baby chicken was brought to school on the next Pet Day, the teacher had the opportunity to help the children learn a new concept.

"How many legs does the chicken have?" she queried. "Is the chicken an animal?"

Some of the children replied yes while others were not so sure.

"It *is* an animal, but it is a different kind of animal. It's a bird," the teacher told them.

The children found this difficult to believe until they looked at the storybook *Are You My Mother?* and saw birds—with two legs.

Sometimes children develop erroneous concepts because of their limited experience. An alert teacher can look for ways to teach new concepts and correct faulty ones.

David watched the baby chick spread its wings. "Look, teacher, it has needles in its wings!"

"David, that is where feathers will come in," answered the teacher. "Those are called quills."

TEACHERS

9. The Teacher Helps Children Solve Their Own Problems

Children gain independence and feelings of self-worth when they solve their own problems. Some children, for example, are so stymied by working a puzzle that they will stop or request a teacher to finish it for them. A good teacher will turn the puzzle pieces so that their places in the puzzle become more apparent. Or, the teacher will hand the pieces to the child one by one and suggest ways the piece can be turned so that the child has success with the task. Requests for help are turned around by saying, "How would you do it?" or "What can you think of?" or "What else could you do?"

10. The Teacher Realizes That Occasionally There Will Be a Child Who Is Unreachable

Some teachers can be very idealistic and believe that no matter what a child's problem is, they can solve it. These teachers put up with excessive aggression, grit their teeth, and try everything. Months roll by and all the techniques such as positive reinforcement or behavior modification are used without results. Still the teacher clings to the hope that next week or next month will be better. Some children must be seen by a psychologist or other professional in order to be helped. Realistic teachers recognize they cannot do everything, and they get help for those children who need it.

11. The Teacher Will Be in Good Health

It is true that older teachers have bad backs and new teachers have a lot of colds. However, a teacher is needed who has stamina, lots of energy, and good mental health. A teacher with serious personal problems and hang-ups that interfere with teaching should not be in a classroom.

12. The Teacher Will Be a Growing Christian Who Is Able to Articulate Faith to Young Children in Terms They Can Understand

Concepts children can understand are:
 a. God loves us.
 b. God has a plan for us.
 c. God has made everything in the world and it is good.

The children experience the faith of teachers because the teachers have an awareness of God which permeates classroom living. John Westerhoff says, "Our children will have faith if we have faith and are faithful" *(Will Our Children Have Faith?* New York: Seabury Press, 1976).

Such a faith shines through as we move from one classroom situation to another.

1. Carrie walked very slowly into the classroom.

Carrie:	My dog died last night.
Teacher:	I am sorry, Carrie. Do you want to sit with me in the rocker and talk about it?
Carrie:	Did he go to heaven?
Teacher:	I don't know what plan God has for dogs, but I do know it is a good plan. God always has a good plan for all of us.

2. The children were watching three small toads that had found their way onto the playground. Suddenly Alan stood up and started to stomp on one. The teacher's arm shot out, restraining the foot from landing on the hapless toad.

"He has a home that he needs to go to, Alan. He is probably hopping there right now. Let's watch and see which way he goes."

There is a reverence for life and an unshakable knowledge that no matter what the situation, God does have a plan and it is a good one.

STEPS IN HIRING

The director's first task will be to put teaching applicants at ease. Having a desk between the director and the applicant creates a physical barrier that imposes a great psychological distance. Two chairs, side by side or at angles to each other, help to promote a relaxed atmosphere.

Small talk is a safe beginning—the weather, where the candidate may be from or went to school. A good lead-in remark for the main part of the interview would be, "Tell me about your background." This invitation enables the prospective teacher to comment about previous experiences with young children. The remark will probably also initiate talk about the applicant's educational background so that the director can ask about a college major and whether courses in child development or early childhood education were included.

Some questions asked by the director will help determine how flexible the new teacher will be. Examples of such questions are:
1. How would you feel if a child wanted to paint more than one picture? Suppose the child wanted to paint five pictures? Fifteen?

2. Suppose you had mixed a container of red paint and one of blue paint for the easel. Tommy says he wants yellow paint. What would you do?
3. You are reading a story. Some children are not paying attention, although they are not creating a disturbance. Would you continue reading?

As the director listens to the applicant's responses to questions about sample classroom situations, an understanding of the person's attitudes and ability to meet children's needs will be gained. Flexible teachers are able to let the children make some decisions for themselves. The more teachers can involve children in decision making, the more self-reliant children become.

In order to discover some of the attitudes the applicant has about bringing Christianity into the classroom, the director might ask:

1. How do you feel about chapel for young children?
2. Would you use Bible study with them?
3. What kinds of prayers do you think should be included as you work with the children each day?

Children learn Christianity best by having it modeled for them. Teachers who can practice Christian living in the classroom in their love, care, and concern for everyone are giving strong lessons in what Christianity is all about.

Simple, heartfelt prayers such as, "Thank you, God, for Michael's new baby brother" and "Thank you, God, for this beautiful day!" are stated in terms that have meaning for young children.

A prospective teacher's grasp of child development would be revealed by the way questions such as the following are answered:

1. Johnny knocks down another child's block tower. How would you handle it?
2. Susie has been watching the children on tricycles for a long time. She says, "Teacher, I want to ride now." What do you do?
3. It is time to go inside from the playground. Your co-teacher starts in with a group. You are the last to come in with a few children. One child refuses to come. What would you do?

Teachers who have not had much experience in working with young children may find such situations bewildering. However, techniques of teaching can be taught by in-service training and by placing a new, inexperienced teacher with more experienced ones.

All the time the interview is being conducted the director will be assessing whether or not the prospective teacher is warm, friendly, outgoing, has a sense of humor, has good eye contact or looks away when talking, and appears at ease. The ability to get along with people will make the teacher's job with parents easier. Teachers need to be able to relate with others and be interested in and accepting of others.

Small children need lots of physical contact. Hugs and laps to sit on are as important to them as nourishing food. During the interview, questions can be asked that will help reveal a teacher's feelings about meeting this need in children.

1. Do you like for children to sit on your lap?
2. Suppose a child wanted to hold your hand a lot. How would you feel about that?

The teacher who drops down to a child's eye level and takes the child's hand while speaking is communicating not only in words but also by touch. Children need an arm around them, a touch on the shoulder, a snuggle. They need physical evidence that they are loved.

The director may want to list on a sheet of paper those areas to be covered in the interview. There might be space after each area where notes could be made. But the director's taking notes during an interview makes some applicants feel uncomfortable. Applicants may feel as if they are taking a test and wonder what is being written. It is best to jot down notes *after* the applicant leaves. These notes will help later, especially if some time elapses before the teaching position is filled. Sometimes persons will apply during the school year at a time when there are no openings. When the time comes to fill positions for September, notes from interviews conducted earlier in the year can be referred to.

Sample

INTERVIEW SHEET

Applicant's name _____ Date _____

Address _____

Phone _____

General impressions:

   Self-assured and poised? _____

   _____

   Warm and friendly? _____

   _____

Work Experience: _____

Adequate background? _____

Knowledge of child development _____

Flexibility _____

Attitudes:
   Physical contact _____

   Christianity _____

Other impressions _____

_____

_____

_____

After the interview, a conducted tour of the school will yield more insight into how this person will fit in with the staff. Comments will indicate whether the teacher's philosophy of education is similar to what is being seen in the classroom. The candidate might say, "I like the way the teachers sit down and talk with the children at snack time," or "I like the way so many choices are offered during free play." These remarks indicate that this teacher will also sit down with the children for snacks and will also offer lots of choices. A comment such as, "Aren't the children cute?" will usually mean that the person has no real grasp of what is going on in the classroom.

It is as important for teachers to work in a school that reflects their own philosophy as it is for a school to find new teachers who will fit in easily. Teachers need to be comfortable with a school's method of operation. Some schools are very structured, with children lining up to go down the hall. Some schools require that parents bring the children to the classroom door. Others have the children let out of cars at the front door. If a prospective teacher is not comfortable with a school's practices, another school should be found. The director will want to make sure the teacher will fit in in order to avoid a situation that is not good for the school or for the new teacher.

Since it sometimes happens that teachers may apply at a school when no job opening is available, the director might ask the applicant about substituting in a classroom. All schools need a supply of persons who can come on short notice if a regular teacher calls in sick.

If an applicant does substitute in the school, the director has an opportunity to see the applicant in action and to do further evaluation. When an opening on the staff occurs, the director will already know how the applicant manages classroom situations. Some of the guesswork of how the applicant might fit in with the rest of the staff and with the school is eliminated.

Sample

JOB DESCRIPTION FOR TEACHERS

1. The teacher will be responsible for the classroom, the curriculum, and the children assigned to the teacher.
2. The teacher will be accountable to the director.
3. The teacher will
   a. develop a schedule and curriculum to fit the needs of the children
   b. make home visits and hold parent conferences
   c. maintain developmental records
   d. work in association with the rest of the staff
   e. inform the director about needed equipment, supplies, and repairs
   f. use positive discipline techniques
   g. attend staff meetings and other events for professional development
   h. attend school-sponsored events such as open house and parent meetings

---

WORKING WITH TEACHERS

New teachers require more supervision than teachers who have been with the preschool for several years. A new teacher, fresh out of school, will often do a good job of planning the activities that are used in the classroom. However, dealing with children's behavior effectively may be difficult and the teacher may turn to the director for help. After new teachers develop effective skills for working with groups, they will need less support from the director. Later the teacher will need a listening ear rather than specific suggestions. A mature teacher moves from needing pats on the back to requiring very little support and encouragement. Some teachers may feel that they want more help from the director. A director must judge how much to give, knowing that a teacher's autonomy develops when the teacher solves problems independent of the director.

Let us look specifically at some of the approaches a director will use to foster growth and independence in teachers.

1. Help the Teacher Arrive at the Solution to a Problem Rather Than Giving the Answer

Teacher: Mark is so disruptive! He interrupts story time every day. He is really bothering me.

Director: What have you tried with him?

Teacher: Jean (co-worker) has tried holding him on her lap.

Director: Do you know what could be going on at his home?

Teacher: His mother says he likes to be babied. He sometimes uses baby talk in class.

Director: How are his peer relationships?

Teacher: The other kids are turned off by his baby talk. They really avoid him.

Director: What does his mother do about the baby talk?

Teacher: The whole family gets on him about it.

Director: It really gets their attention!

Teacher: Say, do you suppose he does it to get attention at school?

Director: You may have put your finger on what his real need is. What do you think can be done to meet his need for more attention?

At this point the teacher's ideas came tumbling forth. She suggested looking for ways to increase his self-esteem and at the same time enhance his value in the eyes of the other four-year-olds. "He needs some jobs!" she ventured. "And strokes for doing them!"

2. Support Teachers and Build Their Self-esteem

Teachers' self-esteem is enhanced first of all by knowing that they work in a good program and that they were chosen out of all the applicants.

As we have noted, new teachers are very unsure of themselves. They may try a theme idea only to find that it was too challenging for the children or that it was too simple and did not generate much interest. They may feel unsure about how to help shy children or aggressive ones. Different lengths of attention spans in the class may pose quite a puzzle to some teachers.

TEACHERS

Each success that teachers have becomes the building block for more success. Teachers have a need for the director to notice they have done well and to give approval. "I like the way you handled that parent conference." "The kids really responded to you at circle time."

Teachers work very hard planning their classroom activities, assembling the needed materials, talking with parents, and leading groups of children with individual learning styles and needs. A director increases the teacher's self-esteem by communicating an awareness of how hard the teacher works.

"You really located a lot of interesting articles to use with your unit on Indians."

"I like the way you have the children sit down on the floor and place a towel on their laps before they hold the guinea pig."

"Mrs. Smith looked so much more relieved after she talked with you."

Self-esteem comes from the knowledge that an individual has done well and from knowing that others, especially the director, are aware of it.

3. Express Requests Positively

By telling people what they can do rather than what they cannot do, we give suggestions for solving problems. Criticism immobilizes people and makes their reactions defensive. Consider how one director dealt with the problem of a storage closet: "This closet is a mess. You certainly aren't very neat. Don't keep it so messy!" Such a way of approaching the problem can only bring about feelings of guilt, frustration, and anger on the teacher's part. The teacher may shout back, "I'd like to see you do better with all there is to do in here every day."

By phrasing the request positively, a director can give a teacher real help in solving the problem. "We could have a rotation system for keeping our closet neat. Each teacher could straighten it once a month."

Other examples of phrasing requests positively are:

"Let's check the church calendar to see if that room is available for a conference," rather than, "Don't use that room for a conference!"

"Let's park away from the building so mothers can park up close" is more effective than, "Teachers can't park next to the building."

"Let's station ourselves on the playground so that a teacher is near the slide and another is near the jungle gym" is better than, "Don't talk together on the playground."

4. Let Teachers Know What Is Expected from Them

Having an experienced teacher in a classroom can lessen a director's work load. Some new teachers instinctively seem to know what to do; others need suggestions to make their teaching function smoothly. The following is a list of expectations that can be discussed with new teachers during an orientation. Copies can be presented first to teachers when they apply at the school. Because many of the suggestions involve the school's philosophy, an orientation discussion helps clarify the expectations.

Sample
EXPECTATIONS OF TEACHERS

1. Teachers need to keep records. Attendance records are needed so that a child's parents can be called if the child is absent. Developmental records are necessary so that end-of-the-year summaries can be written for each child's school record and passed on to the teacher the following year. Developmental records are also invaluable for parent conferences. They may, in addition, be necessary to meet some states' licensing requirements. Record keeping is time-consuming. It is important that teachers understand both its importance and the amount of time it will take.
2. Teachers should always make a count of the number of children present each day. Several times during the day a teacher will again count to make sure that everyone has come in from the playground or that no one has escaped unnoticed through the door. Counting must be done often on field trips.
3. Snack time is a together time, a time for socializing and enjoying each other's company. The teacher sits down at the table with the children rather than standing and talking with co-teachers or aides.
4. The room is in readiness before the children arrive. All the paint is mixed, the manipulatives are out on tables, water is in the water table, and books for story time have been chosen.
5. Each child is given a personal greeting upon arrival at school. Parents are greeted also.
6. Each child is checked for signs of illness and is sent back home if contagious.
7. Parents are encouraged to stay with a child until the child feels comfortable about having the parent leave.
8. Parents are phoned if a child has been absent for more than a day.
9. Parents are made to feel welcome and are treated in a friendly, caring manner.
10. Parents are informed of any accident, injury, or illness.
11. Rooms look better if time is taken for a little tidying, such as pushing chairs up against tables if they are overturned or scattered about the room. Toilets are kept flushed.
12. All teachers help at end-of-the-year cleanup. Equipment is washed, repaired, catalogued, and stored.
13. A child should never be turned over to anyone except the child's parents or those on car pool lists. These lists are posted for easy reference.
14. Teachers should help children remember what they worked on each morning while at school. This helps develop self-esteem and helps with an answer when parents ask, "What did you do today?"
15. Permission slips are obtained from parents whenever the class will be away from school. This includes a walk around the block as well as a longer field trip. Blanket permissions for the whole year are never used. It can be very unsettling for a parent to arrive at school early, perhaps to take the child for a checkup, and find the whole class gone.
16. Teaching pictures are on walls at children's eye level. They are attached with tape rather than thumbtacks.
17. Equipment is in good repair. Broken equipment is taken away to be repaired and not left out in the room.
18. The block center is away from glass windows.
19. Children are allowed to express their feelings, positive as well as negative.
20. Children are allowed to choose their activities.
21. Children are hugged and held as much as they need.

TEACHERS

TEACHERS' NEEDS

In order for teachers to love their profession and stay with a school year after year, a climate in which they can thrive needs to be created. It has little to do with salary, for indeed, this is a field where salaries are very low. Other needs are often more important than salary. Some of these needs center around the following areas:

1. Teachers Need to Be in a School That Reflects Their Own Philosophy of How Children Learn

Some schools are concerned with the whole child; some are more concerned with the children's cognitive or intellectual development. Some are highly structured; some are not. Some schools place a lot of emphasis on motor development. Prospective teachers also can have their own ideas of how children best learn. The school where teachers choose to work must match their philosophy or else they will feel like a square peg in a round hole. When there is a good match of philosophies, the school and the teacher benefit from each other. The teacher has found the proper climate in which to grow.

2. Teachers Need to Be Respected as Individuals with Their Own Unique Teaching Style

Even though teachers believe in their school's philosophy, each one has his or her own individual way of interpreting it. No classroom will be a carbon copy of other classrooms, nor will an individual teacher's way of working with children be exactly the same as that of the teacher next door. For example, one teacher may speak very softly to children; another may be more effervescent. One classroom may contain all bright colors with lots of red and orange on the bulletin boards. Another room will have softer colors such as blues and greens chosen for its bulletin boards. One teacher may be uncomfortable with a lot of overt, active behavior and choose activities that encourage children to sit and work quietly. Teachers who know themselves know the kind of class environment and activities with which they are most comfortable. A good director encourages this uniqueness, knowing this is how teachers thrive.

3. Teachers Need to Know That What They Do Is Important and That They Are Persons of Worth

Parents sometimes share with a teacher that they are glad their child is in her or his classroom. Sometimes they merely think it and never are able to put into words their feelings of gratitude. When they register their children for next year's classes, a question can be included on the application asking why they want their child to continue in school. Such a question will help parents verbalize their appreciation and these responses can be shared with the teachers. Frequently, parents tell the director how much they enjoy having their child with a particular teacher. The director should immediately pass on these compliments. All of us need to know that we are appreciated and that our hard work has not gone unnoticed.

4. Teachers Need Ongoing In-service Training

Teachers want to stretch and grow on the job and be more informed and capable each year than they were the year before. No good teacher is content with doing the same activities the same way year after year. New ideas spark new interest and curiosity, and teachers grow from new ideas. They want and need new ways of presenting material. New ideas in music, art activities, the science table, and the homemaking center will keep a teacher fresh.

Directors have to plan for their teachers' ongoing growth. First of all, there must be money in the budget for professional development. Continuing education might include bringing in an expert for staff meetings as well as enabling teachers to attend workshops in their field. Many excellent workshops are available through the church, the public schools, colleges and universities, and the National Association for the Education of Young Children (and its state and local chapters).

Another way to enable teachers to grow is to choose a text in child development or early childhood education and have the staff study it, chapter by chapter. They can discuss the text at their scheduled staff meetings. Such texts, if they are good, will provoke much discussion. A good book list in the field of child development can be obtained from the National Association for the Education of Young Children, 1834 Connecticut Avenue, N.W., Washington, D.C. 20009. Additional books that elicit interesting discussions for staff meetings are:

Axline, Virginia. *Dibs: In Search of Self.* New York: Ballantine Books, 1976.

Baker, Katherine Read. *Ideas That Work with Young Children.* Washington, D.C., National Association for the Education of Young Children, 1972.

Briggs, Dorothy C. *Your Child's Self-Esteem.* New York: Doubleday, 1975.

Cazden, Courtney B. *Language in Early Childhood Education*, rev. ed. Washington, D.C.: National Association for the Education of Young Children, 1980.

Read, Katherine H. *The Nursery School.* New York: Holt, Rinehart & Winston, 1976.

Smith, Betsy, and Williams, Sara. *Once upon a Year.* Houston: Learning Innovations, 1983.

White, Burton L. *The First Three Years of Life.* Englewood Cliffs, N.J.: Prentice-Hall, 1975.

Another approach for in-service training is to have each teacher take a turn leading the staff meeting and being responsible for a topic of discussion. Probably the one who will benefit the most, in addition to the total staff, will be the person preparing the presentation. Being the discussion leader means analyzing the material and learning it well. In doing so, new ideas are discovered. Opportunities in leading staff meetings will enable some teachers to realize that they really enjoy guiding other adults through a learning process. Their names can be suggested when the school is called for a workshop leader. Such an opportunity allows a teacher to grow professionally.

Staff meetings that are planned for the growth of teachers are excellent ways for them to think through practices in which they might be engaged that are not good learning situations for young children. For example, a staff meeting that has "Outdoor Learning Centers" as its topic may point up all the good learning experiences that can happen on a playground. Teachers who have been using this time to stand in clusters and chat with other teachers may not have considered the playground period as a fertile time for learning. The staff meeting is a positive way to help teachers, rather than a less helpful, negative approach such as calling teachers on the carpet for chatting together on the playground.

Teachers who have a choice in the material that is used for staff meetings will choose what is pertinent to them in their situation. When they choose what is of interest to them, they will be more interested in learning. Teachers need regularly scheduled staff meetings, and once a week is not too often. There are several reasons:
- a. As we have discussed, staff meetings can be training events that keep teachers up-to-date.
- b. Staff meetings give teachers a sense of community.
- c. Teachers learn from each other as they discuss theory and technique.
- d. Staff meetings are a way of making sure that the school's philosophy is the same in every class. The children will profit as they move up through the school, year after year, by being treated in essentially the same way.

5. Teachers Need to Work with Co-teachers and Aides with Whom They Are Compatible

Teachers must feel they are valuable contributors to a team. They need to feel a respect for their co-workers and director. Teachers need help in the classroom. When another teacher is available, there are more eyes, arms, and laps for the children. Having two teachers in a classroom is quite different from getting along with someone who teaches across the hall. Directors must think through staff assignments very carefully, because some people are a good match and others are not. Since no one is perfect, a teacher usually welcomes working with another person who enjoys activities which complement her or his ability. One teacher may be better at home visits and parent conferences. Another may do an excellent job of setting up the classroom for open house with posters that describe the rationale for each activity in class. One teacher may enjoy being in the middle of the action in the block center or in the housekeeping area. Another may prefer sitting down with children as they enjoy quiet art activities such as working with clay. These blends of personalities, as we match people who complement each other, give children and parents a more complete, whole experience.

6. Teachers Need a Director Who Is a Good Role Model

Watching the director talk to parents and work with children in the classroom enables teachers to observe good techniques in action. Requests are phrased positively when talking to children. Words are given for concepts as the children work ("You've painted a *yellow* picture"). Calmness is modeled in the face of a crisis. A good director is not above mopping up spills or fixing a toilet. A new teacher learns from these examples, and experienced teachers see their own styles reinforced. For this reason, boards must choose a director very carefully because others will learn from observing and working with the director. The director should not have a class but be free to work with all the teachers. Nor should the school become big without sufficient office help for the director. The director needs adequate time to spend with the teachers.

7. Teachers Need to Know That They Are Important to Their Director

Teachers should feel that if they quit teaching at the school, their absence would be keenly felt. A loss would exist on the team that makes up the school, and no one could quite fill the shoes. Teachers need to know their director values them. A director's caring will show itself in many ways, such as birthdays planned for, lunches or trips together, a day off given to a teacher on occasion. A director who cares about teachers will remember that they are persons in their own right, usually mothers as well as teachers. They will need to make personal phone calls sometimes and visit their own children's school. Teachers will need a listening ear, someone with whom they can share ideas, and sometimes a shoulder to cry on. A caring relationship is just as important as a professional one.

8. Teachers Need to Know That Their Relationship with Their Director Is Based on Honesty and Trust

Teachers want a director who will always be frank with them. Criticism as well as compliments will be passed on to them because knowing everything a parent feels and says enables a teacher to best deal with a situation and grow from it. Of course, a director will pass on a criticism with kindness, trying to point out to the teacher some of the motivations the parent may have had and thus helping the teacher to still be accepting of the parent. For example, a parent complained to a director that a teacher should not have allowed other children in the bathroom when her child was using the toilet. The parent's overconcern for modesty may well have caused the remark. When the director talked with the teacher about the criticism, both the director and teacher made plans to help the parent understand why an open-door policy is a good one for very young children.

Sometimes parents complain about a teacher's approach with children because of their own insecure feelings. In another example, one parent came to a director with the criticism, "That teacher doesn't control the class. Why doesn't someone spank some of those boys?" As it turned out, the parent's child was having difficulty entering and being a part of the group because of extreme shyness. The teacher was giving the child lots of help in becoming more socially skilled. The parent knew the child was shy and had a desire to have the other children spanked in order to hurry up the process of the acceptance of the child. It is when the director and teacher work together that the most good can come for the child.

Teachers also need to know that a director will stand behind them when a parent comes with a complaint. This shows teachers that the director respects their ability, even when listening to the parent and checking out the problem. A good director tells a parent, "I'm sure the situation was assessed and action taken according to what the teacher thought was best. I'll check into it." This statement readily shows the parent that the director trusts the teacher's judgment. However, the problem is not brushed aside. A director should look into all problems that come up.

When a director does not feel the need to observe in a classroom, trust is shown in the teacher's performance. The director knows the teacher can effectively manage parent conferences and curriculum planning. The director relays that trust to the teacher. When a teacher talks of an upcoming difficult parent conference, the director replies, "I know you can do it." "This child is in good hands," the director confides to a teacher when a new child is enrolled in the class.

TEACHERS

9. Teachers Need to Know That It Is Okay to Say "No" to Some Requests

Teachers will often be asked to undertake a lot of extra volunteer work in addition to their teaching load. Teaching Sunday school in their own church will be requested frequently, as will scouting and raising money for charities. If teachers can manage these extras in addition to a job and family, they should go ahead and participate. However, teaching young children is very demanding work. The teacher may well be drained after an energetic day in the classroom. There is a need to draw the line in accepting more work in order to avoid burnout.

10. Teachers Need Information

New teachers need to have their duties clearly stated along with a job description. They need keys, information about where to find everything, and all printed data on the school. Teachers need access to the children's files, where they can find medical information and write-ups from the teachers whose classes the children were in the previous year. They need test results on children. They also should be informed about any information that affects the school, such as changes in tuition rates, plans for remodeling or expansion, and rules and regulations from licensing agencies. Informed teachers are better decision makers.

Teachers need to know exactly what is expected of them. A school does not simply hire someone and hope for the best. If a teacher is expected to attend parent education programs periodically or make a speech to parents at open house, the teacher needs to know about these expectations. Some state licensing requirements state that teachers must participate in a certain amount of in-service training. The board and director may require attendance at weekly staff meetings. Teachers are helped to meet the expectations that the director and board have of them when those expectations are put in writing.

Teachers who stay with a weekday program year after year are those whose needs are being met. They have a lot of respect for themselves, for their profession, and for their school.

EVALUATION OF TEACHERS

Those who are in business and industry go to great lengths to evaluate personnel. Sometimes the director and board think they must also do this in the preschool. Boards should be informed about teachers' performances because their approval determines whether the teachers will be hired again. It is the director's duty to give this appraisal to the board. The director is the one who is most acutely aware of a teacher's performance in the classroom as a result of seeing that teacher in action throughout the year.

Teachers need to be aware of what they are evaluated on and what the director expects from them (see "Expectations of Teachers," page 72). Evaluations should be based on expectations stated in the job description.

A director's report to a board should cover the following areas:
1. A teacher's relationship with the children
    a. Activities are planned for and carried out that are based on the children's abilities and interests.
    b. Children's self-esteem is enhanced, and a good emotional climate is created in the classroom.
    c. Children are helped with social skills.

2. A teacher's relationship with the children's parents
    a. The teacher regularly reports to parents about their children's progress and works with the parents as partners in the progress of their children.
    b. The teacher helps parents feel at ease at school.
    c. The parents like the teacher.
3. A teacher's relationship with the rest of the staff
    a. As a member of a team, the teacher shares ideas and gives encouragement to others on the team and the staff.
    b. The rest of the staff likes the teacher.
4. The classroom environment
    a. The classroom is inviting and interesting to the children.
    b. Interest centers are changed often enough that the children are always challenged.
    c. The daily schedule meets the children's needs. There is sufficient time for children to participate in interest centers without being rushed through projects that are begun. The daily schedule has active times followed by quiet activities so that children have a change of pace.
5. Program planning
    a. Units and curriculum activities are stimulating and interesting to the children.
    b. Curiosity and creativity are encouraged.
    c. There is much individualized teaching.

When the director reports to the board on the evaluation of teachers, it can be very helpful to graphically illustrate the evaluation. This can be done on a chalkboard which can be erased afterward, or on poster board which can later be thrown away. It is also a good time to remind the board about confidentiality, especially if new members have recently joined.

Here is a sample of what you might include:

Sample
EVALUATION OF TEACHERS

	Teacher 1	Teacher 2	Teacher 3
Relationship with children in class			
Relationship with children's parents			
Relationship with staff			
Classroom environment			
Planning			

TEACHERS

The director usually evaluates teachers with the board when it is time to issue contracts for the next year. However, when working with teachers, evaluation is a continuing process. Part of a director's job is to give ongoing feedback about each of the above areas. She or he will, for example, make it known to the whole staff that planned conferences with parents are expected and are necessary in helping parents understand their children. Staff meetings are planned to help teachers see the value of building self-esteem and learn ways of doing it. Teachers are registered in workshops where they will find new ideas for curriculum. Thus, a good director constantly works toward making good teachers better. Helpful suggestions and encouragement are given throughout the year.

When something happens in the preschool which is not to the children's advantage, a good director will be on top of the situation rather than letting it fester until an evaluation at the end of the year. An example would be a new teacher using too harsh discipline. As soon as the director learns of this, a staff meeting around the topic of classroom environments in which children thrive best would be planned. Suggestions would also be made to the teacher for alternate and more effective ways of relating to children.

Another example would be a new teacher who is having trouble learning to use positive rather than negative suggestions with children. A staff meeting in which all the teachers practice eliminating "no" and "don't" from their vocabulary can help not only the new teacher but all the others. The staff can be divided into groups of two and a worksheet can be handed out. Responses could be verbal with each other. Or, each teacher could fill out the worksheet, then share responses with the total group. The following sample worksheet contains the kinds of statements that could be included.

Sample
WORKSHEET FOR POSITIVE PHRASING

Situation	*Teacher Response**
1. Child is pouring juice on the floor.	"We drink our juice" or "You may pour water at the sand and water table" rather than, "Don't pour the juice on the floor."
2. Child is throwing sand.	"We dig in the sand" rather than, "Don't throw the sand."
3. Child goes out the classroom door.	"We stay in the room" rather than, "Don't go out the door."
4. Children run in the hall.	"We walk" rather than, "Don't run."
5. Child knocks over someone's block tower.	
6. Child dumps box of collage materials.	
7. Child drops jacket on the floor.	

*The teacher responses are examples of possible responses. These responses should be omitted when preparing the worksheet.

THE CHURCH-RELATED PRESCHOOL

Teachers profit from looking at the year's work with the director. Because none of us feels good about being judged by others, the best evaluation is for the director to help a teacher evaluate herself or himself. The focus is not on what the director thinks of the teacher's performance, but rather on how the teacher feels about it.

Two questions a director might ask are:
1. What have you liked best about this year?
2. As you think about next year, what would you like to change or do differently?

The director, too, will have some input about positive aspects of the teacher's year. The director and teacher can perhaps share a laugh about something that went wrong. This kind of evaluation is best done under very relaxed circumstances. When the evaluation process is a positive, nonthreatening experience for the teacher, it is a growth experience.

SOLVING STAFF PROBLEMS

The time when staff problems are apt to occur is when a school is new or when there has been a turnover on the staff. A new school has to develop a philosophy of education with which all can live and in which everyone has had input. New persons coming on the staff bring with them notions about curriculum and schedules that must interact with current methods. It takes time for a new staff member to become part of a team.

When staff conflicts occur, there are several ways a director might respond to the problem:

1. First of all, sleep on it. A director's initial reaction may be one of anger. Hasty decisions should never be made. Take a day or so to think it through.
2. Do not ignore it. Waiting for the problem to disappear will only make it worse.
3. Consider whether the problem can be managed as a learning experience for the whole group in a staff meeting. Discipline and other methods of handling children will be subjects of interest to everyone. At the same time, a teacher who had been very negative with a child might see new and different techniques which would be helpful, without losing face in a confrontation with the director.
4. When a face-to-face confrontation is needed, do it privately with the person involved, with as much gentleness and kindness as possible. There is always the other person's point of view to consider.

It may be necessary on occasion to dismiss a staff member. The foremost reason for terminating a teacher without delay would be harsh, abusive behavior with a child. Hurting a child must never be tolerated. A teacher who spanks, pinches, or yanks a child should be warned and if the behavior is repeated should be terminated without delay. Teachers who belittle children, shame them, or use the put-down should be advised of more acceptable behavior and then released if they are unable to comply.

We may also choose not to renew the contract of a teacher who has personal or emotional problems that affect the quality of teaching. A teacher whose thoughts are miles away or one who breaks out in tears frequently does not belong in a classroom. However, some personal problems, such as the illness or death of a spouse, may be handled with some time off for the teacher. Perhaps a few weeks or a month away will give the teacher time to recover.

We may also choose not to rehire a teacher who does not get along with parents or with other staff members. A teacher with an abrasive personality can mean a year of

TEACHERS

turmoil for the whole school. One who gossips about other staff members, who divides the staff on issues, or who attempts to corral a few teachers to one way of thinking can only bring internal trouble to a program.

Terminating someone or not renewing a contract is never easy. Such action is usually in the best interests of the school as well as giving the teacher an opportunity to find a new school or a new career that better suits the teacher's personality and abilities.

When we have made the decision not to rehire a teacher at contract time, remembering these points will make the conference easier on the director as well as the teacher.

1. Show an understanding of how the teacher feels by accepting feelings.

    "You really were angry with the children. You must have a lot bottled up inside you."

    "Cathy really made you mad on the playground today. I have noticed that you react this way with some of the children."

    "It has been a hard year for you. I know your mind has been on other things."

    "It is hard to talk to little children when you're worrying about someone."

2. Every person is good at something. It may be that teaching little children is not the most suitable career choice for some people. We do them a favor in the long run when we help them out of a situation that is not rewarding or fulfilling for them.

    "I have noticed that you keep such an orderly record of expenses. You must enjoy working with numbers."

    "Your ideas on decorating the teachers' lounge this year were really innovative. Have you ever considered a career in interior decorating?"

3. Offer hope for the future.

    "I know you will find a career that you will enjoy more."

    "A lot of companies are looking for someone with your skills."

It accomplishes nothing if we terminate a teacher by rebukes, criticism, and censure. We must preserve the teacher's dignity so the teacher can look ahead to a productive future elsewhere.

When a director deals with a staff problem, it is best to write a description of the event, the suggestions given, and any other ways in which a solution may have been offered. Documentation of a director's attempts to modify or change behavior of a staff member should be dated and kept. Although most staff problems can be resolved, such documentation may possibly be needed if the director does not rehire a staff member and the board calls the director to task about the situation. These notes also help the director be more objective when making a decision.

WORKING WITH PARENTS

Work with parents begins with their very first phone call to the school for information. Parents will call to find out about hours of operation, tuition, or other facts. They may ask if they can come and visit the school. This first call can be used to tell the parents about the school and also to establish a relationship of openness and welcome. If parents ask if they need an appointment to visit the school, they can be assured that they are welcome to visit at any time. The calendar should be checked to be sure there is not a field trip scheduled that would take the class away from the school, or it may be suggested that the parent come during free-choice time. But the essential point to be made is that the parent is welcome anytime, even for the whole morning.

Schools that set up roadblocks to visiting parents do not develop trust with parents. A parent may wonder what a school may be trying to hide when requests to visit must be bandied about from secretary to director, or if visiting is limited to a certain time or a certain day. Parents who know it is all right to observe the whole program immediately feel more comfortable about placing their child in the school. Parents need to assure themselves that the child will be in a safe environment. They may wonder if anything or anyone will hurt the children. They want to see for themselves if the teachers treat children well with plenty of loving patience. Last, they are interested in how the school will expand their child's curiosity and ability.

The feeling of welcome is again established by allowing the visitor plenty of time. The invitation to sit down and have a cup of coffee relaxes a parent and invites questions about the school. If we suggest, "Tell me about your child," the parent feels our interest and a good rapport is established.

A tour of all the classes, not just the one the child will attend, again allows a parent to feel comfortable with the school. This tour enables the parent to see what kinds of activities await children during each succeeding year and which teachers they might have as they move from one class to another. Most preschoolers are in the program from two to four years, depending on how young they are when they begin. Parents want to feel not only that each year will offer new challenges, but also that the same philosophy of education will be found in all the classes. For example, if the school's approach to art activities is for children to enjoy the experiences of the different media, such as feeling and pounding clay and making large motions in finger paint rather than making something to take home, parents will want to know that the same approach to art will be evident in the groups of four- and five-year-olds as well as in the classes of three-year-olds.

When parents are given a tour of the school, an explanation of what they are seeing makes the visit more meaningful for them. Three-year-olds tend to fill every hole in a pegboard randomly, for example, while four-year-olds make patterns as they work with pegs and pegboards. A lot of parents may not have thought about differences between three- and four-year-olds. Older two-year-olds and young threes enjoy playing near each other without much interaction (parallel play), while fours enjoy dramatic play with assigned roles ("You be the gas station guy, and I'll drive up here!").

Explaining to prospective parents how discipline is handled in the school also puts them at ease. For them to see positive discipline in action when they tour the school helps them know that their children will be treated kindly and lovingly. For example, as they watch a teacher work with two children, one of whom has snatched a car away from another, they hear the teacher say as the car is restored to its owner, "Bobbie is using the car now. It is his turn. Tell him you would like to have it when he is finished." Parents can see for themselves how effective this approach is.

Parents are very concerned about finding a school where punitive discipline will not be used. The types of discipline a school utilizes should always be discussed when parents visit. Some parents may not even ask, but all of them will certainly wonder about it. Some will venture, "What would you do if a child were really behaving badly?" The parent needs assurance that the worst that could happen would be that the teacher would hold the child until the child is in control and calm again. Parents want to know that their children will not be spanked or hurt in any way. They should be told how positive redirection is the most effective way of working with children.

Parents frequently remark that they want to enroll their child because "This is the best school in town," or "We've heard so many good things about this program!" The preschool is offering a service the staff believes in. They should not hesitate to agree with the parents about the quality of the school. When the staff has no reservations about the school being an excellent environment for young children, the enthusiasm convinces others. Just as a salesman must completely believe in the superiority of the brand being sold before others can be convinced of its quality, so must the staff be convinced not only of the value of preschool education but also of the school's worth. In effect, the staff members of a preschool are the salespersons of the services of the school.

When a teacher visits with a child and family in the home, the child is helped to accept the teacher. Perhaps the child sees the parent plan for the visit by preparing a snack. The youngster sees the parent welcome the teacher into the home as a friend. The child begins to think, "Dad likes this person, so I will too." The home visit helps the child feel comfortable with the teacher. It establishes a good working relationship between the child, the parents, and the teacher.

Parents like to be told some basic information during this first home visit. Much of this may seem obvious. It may be included in the parent handbook or other literature distributed by the school. Sadly, not all parents read the printed material. This information also could be communicated verbally in a parent orientation. Information may include:

1. *The Kind of Clothing Children Should Wear to School*

Some parents think the term *school clothes* means party dresses or other fancy attire. Children who will be enjoying clay, paint, glue, water play, sand, tricycle riding, and climbing need old clothes. Schools regularly buy washable paints to use, which just as regularly do not always wash out of clothing, even if children are swathed in aprons.

Children sometimes come to school in cowboy boots or shiny patent leather "Mary Janes" with slick leather soles. Parents may need a reminder to send children in rubber-soled shoes in which they can climb easily and which will prevent them from sliding as they walk (and sometimes run) down long church halls.

2. *The Daily Schedule*

When teachers go over their daily schedule with parents, it becomes easier for them to see the value of being on time. The day may begin with a circle time, and children do not like to arrive in the middle of a story or a song. It may begin with a free-choice time. It is no fun for a child to walk into a room and find a favorite doll already being used or all the easels already taken.

Knowing the daily schedule helps a parent plan for lunch (the parent will be aware of when juice and snack are served). Knowing if playground time is early or late in the morning helps a parent know how heavy an outer wrap the child will need.

Parents appreciate learning that their child will probably come home tired. The morning will be full of many varied activities, and most children need a good lunch and a nap afterward.

3. The Teacher's Goals for the Year

Teachers have a plan for the children's growth during the school year. They will encourage social skills by helping children learn to tell one another about their wants and feelings. Teachers plan for the development of concepts by the kinds of activities that are offered. Language skills are enhanced through group games, finger plays, and stories that are made up by the children. Parents will appreciate knowing the broader scope of a teacher's goals. There is so much more to preschool than just learning colors and numbers.

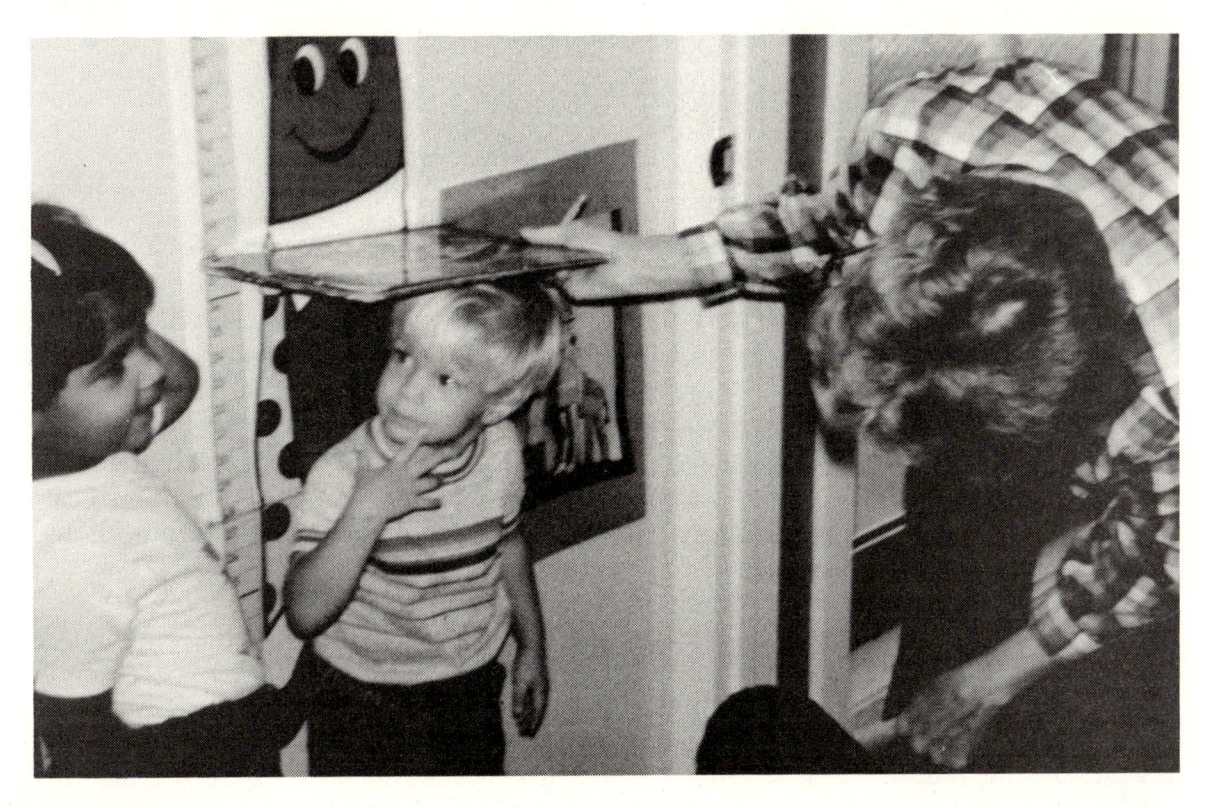

4. Parking

Some churches are not blessed with good parking facilities. Suggestions for the safest places to park will be welcome. Parents may also have to be reminded that some parking spots are reserved for church staff, if this is the practice at your church. Those who are honored with a reserved place may not appreciate sharing it with a parent, and sometimes parents do not realize that ministers work during the week as well as on Sundays. A parent may also think "I will just be a minute" and run inside with the child, but end up having an interesting conversation or two in the hall. Thus, the car is parked much longer than anticipated, and the owner of the reserved place arrives to find the place taken. Setting clear guidelines for parking will help keep problems at a minimum between church members and school parents.

Also included should be a reminder that parents are to bring children to the classroom doors. Dropping a child off at the curb or in the parking lot is not in the best interest of the child's safety.

5. Change of Clothing

Having a change of clothing sent to school may confuse some parents. They may think their child has been toilet trained for a long time and should not need spare clothing at school. However, teachers can point out that there are other kinds of accidents where dry clothing is needed. Children may spill juice, wash hands all the way to the elbows or shoulders, or become so engrossed in the feel of finger paint that they try it out on their faces or arms. Even school aprons cannot cover everything.

6. How Birthdays Are Celebrated

A discussion of the school's guidelines on birthdays will enable parents to know how they can help with the celebration. Some parents may want to do too much and send fancy foods or great quantities of food. They may even suggest entertainment. Preschoolers do want to feel special on their birthdays but do not need to be overwhelmed. Cupcakes sent from home and the singing of "Happy Birthday" by one's classmates will be all that most of the children can handle. Some schools have a felt "cake" that goes up on the flannel board on birthdays and the birthday child gets to put up the appropriate number of candles. Another school may use a stuffed round pillow that has been decorated with lace to resemble a cake. This pillow is placed on the table at snack time. One teacher may use a poster which the class draws upon and decorates for the birthday child. These activities may seem simple by adult standards, but are just enough of a celebration for a three-, four-, or five-year-old.

It is best to assume that parents do not know the above information. By talking about it, parents have the opportunity to ask questions. A good home visit should always include asking parents if they have any questions. This begins the year with good communication.

An excellent pamphlet is *Three to Six: Your Child Starts to School* by James Hymes. It is available from Public Affairs Pamphlets, 381 Park Avenue South, New York, New York 10016, at a very nominal cost. One of these pamphlets, presented to each new parent during the home visit, will help parents know what to expect from their child's preschool experience.

TEACHER-PARENT CONFERENCES

> First tell them about what you are going to tell them, then tell them, then tell them what you have told them.
> —Author unknown

Some parents approach a teacher-parent conference with feelings of apprehension. They are not certain how the teacher reacts to their child. They may wonder if the teacher actually likes their child, sees the child as being smart, or will think they have done a good job as parents. This will probably be their first experience with a conference, and they want it to go well. A teacher can help parents relax at the beginning by briefly stating the agenda. "Today I would like to talk about Michael's social development as well as his intellectual and physical development." Giving the parents a copy of the areas to be talked about will also help parents relax.

Sample
EVALUATION OF PROGRESS

1. Language development
    How have speech patterns changed?
2. Intellectual development
    Does the child:
       have a sense of curiosity?
       speak in whole sentences?
       know basic colors and shapes?
    What number concepts does the child have?
    How long is the child's attention span?
3. Emotional development
    Is the child basically well adjusted?
    How are stress and change handled?
    Does the child seem to be happy? friendly?
    How are problems solved?
4. Self-esteem
    Does the child try new activities?
    Is the child confident? independent?
5. Social skills
    How well does the child get along with other children at school?
    Can the child deal with other children on a verbal level?
    What kind of place does the child enjoy in the group?
6. Spiritual development
    Does the child:
       show love for others as well as receive it?
       know that prayer is talking to God?
       know that God made the world and has a plan for everything?
7. Physical health
    Has the child:
       missed much school?
       had a stuffy or runny nose most of the year?
       seemed to have difficulty seeing or hearing?
       seemed to be in good health?
8. Physical development
    How is the child's gross motor coordination?
       fine motor coordination?
9. Other comments

This form is used as a guide for conversation. It is not meant to be filled out in writing. If it were filled out, parents would feel that the teacher's views are less likely to change. Any kind of written report, such as report cards, gives authenticity to teachers' value judgments. Parents think the way their child is at this moment is the way the child will always be. Information presented during a conference can be tempered by the way we present it. "Martin does have a hard time now with some eye-hand coordination activities, but I am sure his coordination will develop with time. After all, he is one of the youngest in this class." Helping parents understand a developmental point of view is far different from sending a report that simply says the child is lagging in eye-hand coordination.

A good parent conference begins with the teacher planning ahead of time what will be said. Thinking through each area of growth and planning to give examples when talking with the parents will be helpful. Keeping a file of examples of each child's artwork so that growth in creativity during the year can be explored with parents is useful. The teacher refers to notes that have been jotted down about the important happenings in each child's day-to-day experiences. Here is an example of such a log kept by a teacher.

Sept. 19—Tommy's mother continued to sit in the hall sewing, and Tommy checked occasionally to see if she were there.

Sept. 23—Tommy told his mother good-bye this morning, and she left for the first time. She returned a half hour before school was out. He asked when she was coming for him when he was on the playground.

Oct. 2—Tommy and Jennifer washed their dolls' hair together. This was the first time he played with another child.

Oct. 20—Tommy joined Michael and Stan in the rocking boat.

Such examples help parents see the ongoing process of development. With good teachers available to guide children in their steps toward independence, growth is sure and progress is easy to follow.

A good parent conference always begins on a positive note. The teacher talks first about the most likable qualities a child has.

"I am really enjoying Kristen's comments when we have story time. She sees many things in the pictures that aren't obvious to the other children."

"Charlie is a real organizer. He lined everyone up to go up the steps of the slide."

"Billy loves the block corner. His buildings are intricate and well thought out."

"Laura has a beautiful smile."

Sometimes these insights of teachers are new to parents and help them see their children in a different light. By seeing that others can find much to like in their child, parents become even more accepting than they normally are. The more good qualities parents believe a child has, the more they are likely to share these thoughts with the child, thus increasing the child's self-esteem.

By pointing out a child's good attributes to parents, the parent is helped to be more accepting of the child. When parents see that teachers value their child, they can also see more to value.

"I liked the way Kathy painted today. She knew exactly the way she wanted the pictures to look and made them that way."

The message to Kathy's parents is that her paintings are not just random scribbles, but are well thought out and organized.

A good parent conference always should end on an upbeat note, summing up the child's strengths. "Libby's prereading skills and social development are far along. She will be ready for kindergarten next September."

At no time, however, should a teacher be less than honest with a parent. If there is a concern about a child, this should be reported as well. A teacher has seen scores of children over the years and has become adept at spotting problems. Even though the teacher is not a diagnostician, she or he has a feel for knowing when children are not doing well. None of us likes to tell a parent about a child who is having problems, but in doing so we take the first step in getting real help for the child. Some indicators of children in trouble are:

1. Children who have much shorter attention spans than all the others in the class. These children may have difficulty carrying through a project to its finish and flit from one activity to another.
2. Children with a peculiar gait or posturing such as always tilting the head to one side, or looking at a storybook with the head on one arm, thus covering one eye.
3. The unusually shy child who pulls away from most social contacts.
4. The unusually aggressive child who consistently hits, bites, and hurts others.
5. A child who regularly has a bowel movement in clothes rather than in the toilet.
6. Excessive fearfulness.
7. The overly solicitous, compliant child who may "mother" other children or continually clean and straighten up the room. Also, children who regularly report to the teacher about other children's misdeeds.

Most parents want to do what is best for their child and will follow through in getting professional help. It is best to suggest several names of appropriate professionals rather than just one, thus giving parents a choice.

However, some parents find it very hard to believe that their child may have a problem and oppose suggestions to take the child for an evaluation. Or, they will check with their pediatrician who might say, "He'll grow out of it." These parents may even change schools because it is too painful to see a teacher day after day, knowing that they are resisting the teacher's suggestions. We can only hope that if the parents do go elsewhere, the next school will be just as candid and the parents will then summon the courage needed to get help. Teachers should refrain from passing judgment and should support parents as best they can with whatever decision the parents make.

Many preschools plan for parent conferences by scheduling one early in the fall and one late in the spring. The fall conference becomes a data-gathering time for the teacher to facilitate effectively working with the child throughout the year. What is the child like at home? What are the child's favorite toys? Does the child have favorite stories? Has the child ever had a group experience before? Does the child have playmates? How does the child feel about school? How can the school best help the child? The teacher collects information while the parents do most of the talking.

Spring conferences are a summary of the year's growth. Parents may find it helpful if they are invited to school to observe their child's class for the whole morning preceding the conference. They can be handed the conference sheet (see "Evaluation of Progress") with the growth areas listed so they will know ahead of time the topics that will be covered during the conference. Teachers can use examples from the morning's activities to illustrate to parents in a graphic way how the child has changed over the year.

"Remember how fearful Todd was last fall about making friends? Now he is in the middle of the action every day, just like he was this morning."

"Annette's pictures have changed from the scribbling stage last fall to really looking like what they represent. That was an interesting house she painted this morning."

Conferences can be both planned and unplanned. When a parent brings a child to school or picks the child up to go home, a few words with the teacher at the door can be valuable both for the teacher and the parent.

"Kevin was up late last night when his cousin visited and didn't want to get up this morning. He may be cranky from lack of sleep."

"Marsha went to the bathroom a lot this morning. You may want to keep track of that this afternoon. An infection may be starting."

"Frances worked all morning on this collage for you. I am sure you will want to hang it on the refrigerator."

"Todd told us last night at bedtime that he was going to work with the Bristle Blocks as soon as he came to school."

"I had to put Michelle in the back seat of the car on the way to school. She and Sarah argued all the way here."

These mini-conferences at the classroom door are valuable exchanges, enlightening both teacher and parent. They help a parent feel comfortable about leaving a child and also are a valuable aid in learning what is normal behavior on the part of children.

Occasionally, a parent will ask questions at the classroom door that a teacher may hesitate to answer in front of the child. Most children are well aware of what their teacher thinks of them. If they hear a teacher answer, "I'll call you about that later," the child may wonder what the teacher plans to tell the parent. The child wonders what is wrong. Not knowing is worse than knowing. It would be much better for the teacher to let the child hear the answer, especially if the teacher can incorporate hope that the child will eventually overcome any problem with which the parent is concerned. For example, if a parent asks, "Did he hit anyone today?" the teacher can demonstrate belief in the child's progress with a statement such as, "He felt angry only once and we talked about his using words when he feels angry. Soon he will be able to tell the children how he feels instead of hitting." Such an answer shows both the child and the parent that the teacher believes in the child's ability to solve the problem.

The kinds of comments at the classroom door that worry teachers are disparaging remarks by parents, such as:

"I don't want to put that drippy, messy picture in my car. Can't you leave it at school?"

"Why can't you take your coat off like that little girl can?"

"Stop that whimpering! You've got to stay at school because I am due at a meeting."

It is easy to see how parents might not want a picture that is dripping with glue or paint or why some parents are impatient with their children. We adults crowd so much into a day that a dawdling child can make us short-tempered. Teachers can accept the parents' feelings and at the same time suggest ways to handle the situation that will help the child preserve self-esteem.

"Some newspapers around that picture might keep it from dripping. Alan worked so hard on it and is very proud of it. Perhaps after it is dry you can find a spot on the refrigerator to hang it."

"Mommy is in a hurry to leave this morning, Claire. Can I help you with your coat? It's hard to take it off when you have on such a thick sweater."

"Come with me, Martin. Daddy is going to work, but he will be back. I know you'll miss him. In the meantime I will take care of you. Let's see. Do you think Bunny needs feeding?"

When we accept the feelings of parents, they think, "That teacher really understands!" When we also show the child that we understand the reasons for behavior and offer suggestions for solving problems, the child will feel less rejected by the parent's remark.

CONFIDENTIALITY

Most teachers are aware of the need for confidentiality and would never consider talking about one family to another. All the staff must be on guard against even mentioning the name of another child to a parent. Let us look at the following illustration. In it the teacher is reporting to a parent when the child is picked up from school about an accident that has occurred.

"Timmy has a small cut on his knee, Mrs. Elkins. Jeb happened to be running and accidentally gave Tim a shove. We've cleaned his knee and put a bandage on it."

Once home, Mrs. Elkins becomes upset over the reported shove and phones Jeb's mother, accusing her of not controlling her child. How much better it would have been if the teacher had reported the incident without naming anyone!

"Timmy has a small cut on his knee, Mrs. Elkins. Another child happened to be running and accidentally gave Tim a shove."

When teachers develop friendships with parents, the need for confidentiality may sometimes be forgotten. It is for this reason that teachers can be friendly with parents but should not seek to make any a close friend. When close friendships develop between a teacher and a parent, other parents might wonder what is being said about their own children.

NOTES THAT GO HOME

Directors send many communications home. These notes cover a variety of topics, such as information about next year's registration, when the next school holiday is, or a newsletter about activities at the school. They can inform as well as educate.

Phrasing requests positively can produce better results. Consider the impact of the following two notes.

Dear Parents,

It has come to our attention that people have been parking cars on the grass in front of the church. Please don't park on the grass. Tulip bulbs have been planted there.

Thank you,

Dear Parents,

We know everyone would like to park as near as possible to the front door. However, some of our mothers have planted tulip bulbs all across the front of the church. Please park in a designated parking space. We'll all enjoy the tulips this spring.

Thank you,

Telling parents where they can park is more effective than saying where they cannot park.

Some communications can educate parents and help them be better parents with their children.

Dear Parents:

We know you and your children will have a wonderful Christmas and that you are building and carrying on family traditions. We would like to share a few of our thoughts with you about a wish we have for every child.

We know you love your children; we also know that they will have many gifts at Christmas. It is our hope that you also make a gift of time for each of these little ones. Each child needs time alone with parents. Not time shared with other children in the family; not time while you are also busy cooking or sorting laundry. Not time at dinner which is shared with others in the family. Not time while the child is being dressed or taught. A child needs ten, fifteen, or thirty minutes a day when mommy or daddy can be alone with the child to read, play, talk, or just hold the child closely. Perhaps the phone could even be off the hook for that long.

The child who knows there is a definite time each day that can be considered his or hers does not have to fight continuously for attention. Disciplinary problems are lessened because the child feels valued as an individual. Best of all, essential lines of communication are established that will pay off in later years.

Merry Christmas!

PARENT MEETINGS

If one of the goals of our school is to provide a ministry to children and their families, then what kind of parent involvement can we offer? We should start where our families have interests and needs. We can determine this with a questionnaire at the beginning of each school year, because each year brings new families with new needs and interests.

Good programs, such as evening meetings, morning mothers' groups, and workshops of several weeks' duration, are usually well attended if the subject matter is of interest to parents. Some possible topics are:

Discipline
Learning Disabilities
Understanding Children's Behavior
Developing Children's Self-Esteem
The Effects of Television on Young Children
How to Tell When a Child Is Ready for Kindergarten
Jealousy of the New Baby

Planning for families to have fun together also strengthens them. Many fathers and mothers of young children live far away from any other relatives. Their neighbors may

WORKING WITH PARENTS

Sample

PARENT PROGRAM QUESTIONNAIRE

Our school has always offered interesting programs for parents during the school year. These programs are based on your interests. Please take a few minutes to share your ideas with us.

1. Our family would enjoy attending several social events.   Yes _____   No _____

2. What kind of social event would you enjoy?
   _____
   _____

3. We would like to attend parent meetings.   Yes _____   No _____

4. Please indicate some topics in which you would be interested.
   _____
   _____

5. Would you enjoy hobby classes?   Yes ____   No ____

6. If yes, please tell us your interests.
   _____
   _____

7. Any other ideas for programs?
   _____
   _____

---

move frequently. A weekday program can provide an "extended" family where parents come to know each other as friends. Opportunities for friendships develop when the preschool and church together offer sewing classes, exercise classes, Bible study, and sack lunch and talk sessions. A yearly or twice-yearly picnic enables school families to have fun together. Parents will also get to know each other when they work on committees that plan school functions.

Good weekday programs for children also are good programs for families. We want parents to feel that they are always welcome and that we value their suggestions and their interest. Without working with them, we cannot hope to accomplish as much with the children who are entrusted to us.

Many parents want to become involved with their children's school. They bring their time, talents, and interest, and a weekday program needs them as much as they need to be a part of the program. Some schools form a parents' group to involve parents in decisions about the kinds of educational meetings and social events that will be offered during the year.

Parents can be involved in fund raising, substituting in the classroom, driving for field trips, and bringing their special interests to school. Some parents enjoy conducting a cooking day with the children; others might be willing to sing or play the guitar in class;

still others might share a hobby. One father, for example, brought his skis, boots, and poles to his daughter's class and gave the children an opportunity to put their feet in the boots. Another parent brought a weaving loom; another brought a cider press. Work days can be scheduled so that playground and indoor equipment are constructed or repaired. The more the weekday program can involve parents, the more they will feel a part of the total program.

Problems arise when parents sense that they are intruders. Some teachers give parents the impression that they are a hindrance to the learning process or that it is an imposition upon the teacher's time when they ask questions. When parents are made to feel unwanted, anger and resentment surface as criticism of the teachers or the program.

Parents feel more worthwhile when they know they are valued. They are affirmed when directors and teachers recognize the parent is doing a good job of parenting.

"Jodie told us about the night-light you got for her. You really know how to respond to her fears."

"I like the way you let Martin choose the clothes he wears to school. You are helping him become self-reliant when you let him make choices."

Helping parents feel that they are a vital part of the school's program is an ongoing process. It consists not only of big events such as conferences and parent meetings but of everyday events—a cheery greeting at the door, a note or phone call about something interesting that happened at school, and the offer of a cup of coffee when a parent stops by the office to pay tuition.

The staff and parents are partners in the exciting process of helping young children develop to their fullest potential.

CONCLUSION

Good weekday programs do not just happen. Even though a church may spend a great deal of money and time setting up the program, there is no assurance that money and time represent the chief ingredients for excellence. Rather, the Christlike values of love and caring, turning the other cheek, and doing unto others as you would have them do unto you decide the future of the school. If respecting one another's dignity and helping one another develop self-esteem are practiced, not only by teachers with children and parents, but by the director with teachers, the board with the director, and the church staff with the board, then the whole congregation benefits by seeing Christianity in action. Parents cannot help but want their children in school where the message is "We care."

In a society that is becoming increasingly lax in morality and where our public schools offer little that meets a child's spiritual needs, the necessity for churches to open their doors with weekday programs for children becomes more acute with each passing year.

SUGGESTED READING

Note: Some of the books that we are suggesting may not be available in your local bookstore. You are encouraged to find the books in your public library and use them to help you as the program in your church is developed.

Anderson, Phoebe M. *3's in the Christian Community.* Boston: United Church Press, 1969.
Baruch, Dorothy W. *New Ways in Discipline.* New York: McGraw-Hill, 1949.
Briggs, Dorothy C. *Your Child's Self-Esteem.* New York: Doubleday, 1975.
Cherry, Clare, et al. *Nursery School Management Guide.* Fearon, Belmont, Calif.: Lear Siegler, 1973.
Couch, Robert A. *Church Weekday Early Education Administrative Guide.* Nashville: Convention Press, 1980.
Gilkerson, Elizabeth. *Teacher-Child-Parent Relationships Bulletin.* Early Childhood Education Council of New York, 1972.
Ilg, Frances L., and Ames, Louise Bates. *Child Behavior,* rev. ed. New York: Harper & Row, 1981.
Jorde, Paula. *Avoiding Burnout.* Washington, D.C.: Acropolis Books, 1982.
Kamii, Constance, and De Vries, Rheta. *Physical Knowledge in Preschool Education.* Englewood Cliffs, N.J.: Prentice-Hall, 1978.
Katz, Lilian G. "Challenges to Early Childhood Educators," *Young Children.* Washington, D.C.: National Association for the Education of Young Children, May 1977.

La Crosse, E. Robert. "Thoughts for New Administrators," *Young Children*. Washington, D.C.: National Association for the Education of Young Children, September 1977.
Lindner, Eileen W., et al. *When Churches Mind the Children*. Ypsilanti, Mich.: The High/Scope Press, 1983.
McQuoid, Barbara C. "What Does It Mean to Be a Church Related Preschool?" *Young Children*. Washington, D.C.: National Association for the Education of Young Children, July 1983.
Pitcher, Evelyn, and Ames, Louise Bates. *The Guidance Nursery School*. New York: Harper & Row, 1975.
Read, Katherine H. *The Nursery School*. New York: Holt, Rinehart & Winston, 1976.
Schaller, Lyle E. *Effective Church Planning*. Nashville: Abingdon Press, 1979.
Stone, Jeannette Golambos. *A Guide to Discipline*. Washington, D.C.: National Association for the Education of Young Children, 1979.
Thomas, Gloria V. *Weekday Ministries Resource Book*. Nashville: Graded Press, 1979.
White, Burton L. *The First Three Years of Life*. Englewood Cliffs, N.J.: Prentice-Hall, 1975.
Wilkinson, Henrietta. "Church Options for Day Care." Booklet published for Joint Educational Development. Philadelphia: Geneva Press, 1973.